Cover Image: Clockwise from the top: marquee, *Palmetto Theater* in Hampton, *Strand Theater* in Georgetown, and *PIX Theater* in Rock Hill.

We thank the many citizens of South Carolina's cities and towns who opened their hearts to us as we traveled across the state. This is really their story. You will meet most of them as you read the book. Others, including librarians, local historians, and staff members of Chambers of Commerce, Historical Societies, archives, newspapers and museums are not individually credited but are sincerely appreciated. We could not have written this book without their generous help.

To all we met, talked with on the phone, and corresponded with over the past ten years, we say, *"Thank you."*

A Small Disclaimer

The information in this book is drawn from our research beginning in 2002. These old theaters disappear from time to time. The information, images and stories appearing in this book are as we recorded them at the time.

Movie Theaters of South Carolina © 2012

THE AUTHORS

JOHN R. COLES

John R. Coles is a graduate of the University of South Carolina, where he earned a master's degree in Media Arts.

After four years in the United States Air Force, he worked as a film animator for South Carolina Educational Television in Columbia. In 1970, he became Director of Media for the Chester County Schools.

In 1973, he began teaching in the Media Arts Department at the University of South Carolina. During his college years, he was a member of a locally successful rockabilly band, *Uncle John's Band*. In 1980, he moved to Charleston, where he managed The Charleston Adventure Theatre, a multi-media theatre for tourists.

He was a member of the Board of Directors of *Friends of The Riviera*, a group formed to save the art deco Riviera Theatre in Charleston.

MARK C. TIEDJE

Mark C. Tiedje is a graduate of Rollins College in Winter Park, Florida, where he earned a degree in technical theatre.

He worked as Technical Director at WFTV, Channel 9, in Orlando, Florida. During his college years, he worked in summer stock with The Valley Players, in Holyoke, Massachusetts, and as an usher at the Daytona Theatre in Daytona Beach, Florida.

In 1970, he moved to Charleston, South Carolina, where he was Director of Promotion and Publicity at both WCBD-TV, Channel 2, and WCIV-TV, Channel 4. He recently retired from the College of Charleston, where he was Media Relations Coordinator for the School of the Arts.

He is a member of the Theatre Historic Society (THS), American Theatre Organ Society (ATOS), and a former member of the International Alliance of Theatrical Stage Employees (IATSE) for sixteen years.

Their book, *Movie Theaters of Charleston,* was published in 2009.

CONTENTS

THANK YOU

Contributing Writers

John A. Armistead
Don Fortner
Wilmont Berry
Robert D. McJunkin
Robert W. Ratterree, Sr.
J.T. Green, III
Joe L. Jones
Suzannah Smith Miles
Carol B. Barker
Dr. Robert E. Holman

Interviews

Emily Padgett
Gayle and Thad McCullough
Henry Clinkscales
Mary and Clyde Hudson
Myra Shaffer
Alice and Edward Eatmon
Kent Daniels
Nelson Parker
Jane Britt
Henry Belk Cook
Cindy and John Corley
Andrew J. Daley
Mildred Higgins
Mrs. Helmer Abrams
Gerald Bratcher

Special Material

Bob Grenko
David J. Suggs
Faye Rentz
Gretchen Roepke
Pat Doyle
Debby Summey
Bill Greene
Brian Petit
Francis B. Kerr, Jr.
Mrs. Malcolm L. Marion
Marion Peter Holt
William T. Goldfinch
Mona Burris Dukes
Mayor "Bubba" McElveen
Paul Finnican
Jack Daley

INTRODUCTION

Have a "Chilly Dilly" or a bag of boiled peanuts. Meet the "town reader" and the man who got free tickets because he had an infectuous laugh. Learn what you should never do if the wood stove throws too much light on the screen. Pray for the troops, get trapped in the backseat of a car with Betty Grable, or save on your heating bill. All of these things are what makes the history of South Carolina's movie theaters a unique story. All of this can be found in the pages that follow.

At the peak of the movie palace building boom in 1930, the entire state of South Carolina had a smaller population than the city of Philadelphia. It just didn't have the dense polulation centers to support a grand movie palace.

What South Carolina did have was a widely dispersed rural population who wanted to enjoy the movies just like everyone else. When the executives of major exhibition companies like Paramount Publix failed to provide luxurious movie palaces in South Carolina, local entrepreneurs stepped up and built small theaters in almost every town across the state. The result is a rich heritage of local movie theaters, the people who built them and the people who attended them.

From around 1900 to 1915, seeing opportunity in the growing popularity of motion pictures, clever and ambitious people leased empty store fronts on busy streets in South Carolina, and set up penny arcades and small theaters to satisfy the curious.

Other more adventurous people loaded projection equipment and assorted reels of film in a car or truck and traveled the state's dusty roads, setting up theaters wherever a crowd could be gathered. Sometimes the films were shown in a local auditorium. Sometimes the images were projected on the side of a farmer's barn.

By the 1910s, audiences had grown tired of seeing reels of unrelated scenes. The first picture plays appeared. These were complete stories taking several reels of film. People everywhere were drawn to this new form of entertainment. An industry grew to satisfy the demand.

As the motion picture industry grew, film distribution companies and theater chains evolved. They served the larger markets and ignored the less profitable rural areas of the country.

The movie business grew and prospered in South Carolina in the 1920s because a relatively small group of industrious and passionate people invested in their local communities and brought the movies to eager local patrons.

People who lived on farms traveled to the nearest town to see the popular movies of the day. In 1929, silent picture plays were replaced by "Talkies" and theaters had to be refitted with sound equipment. Local theater owners built larger theaters and opened theaters in smaller communities.

In the late 1940s, local theater owners, following a national trend, opened drive-in theaters all across South Carolina. But, a new novelty was emerging that pulled audiences away from the movie theaters. Television appeared in South Carolina and ticket sales at the local movie theater began to decline.

With declining ticket sales, profits eroded. Theater owners were less able to maintain the auditoriums and equipment. The theaters began to show their age.

In the 1960s, shopping malls appeared to serve the growing suburban areas. Most of these malls offered new "twin" theaters. Many single-screen theaters were sold to consolidated theater circuits. These larger companies, usually located out of state, "twin-ed" some of the old large movie houses. The unprofitable ones were closed.

Fewer people were going to the single-screen theaters of their city's downtown commercial district. That same commercial district was losing local shops to the larger national retail chains.

In the 1970s and 1980s, most of the industrial mills closed as manufacturing moved overseas. The brightly lit marquees of South Carolina's single screen theaters were turned off. It was a grand adventure, but it was over.

Driving through the small towns in South Carolina, it's hard to imagine the busy crowded streets that once welcomed shoppers and theater patrons in earlier times.

Over the past twenty years, we traveled across South Carolina, asking local citizens to share memories of their hometown movie theaters. We gathered photographs, searched old newspapers, and explored collections in local historical societies and museums.

Many times we were guided to the town's unofficial historian. This was often an older local resident who remembered every minor detail of the town's history.

We had many pleasant afternoons, talking with residents over lunch at local cafes and restaurants. In the pages that follow, we hope to share the laughter, joy, excitement, and wonder that we enjoyed. We can't possibly share it all, but we will endeavor to share the best.

Over the course of our journeys across and around this amazing state, we have encountered some truly wonderful individuals. Some sections in this book are alive and exciting because of their input. Some trails we followed simply fizzled out. We know we missed some interesting and entertaining stories along the way.

We have dug as deeply as we could. We have taken our mission seriously, but always looked for the joy to be found. Like any endeavor, this book is a combination of hard work and simple good luck.

We realize now, that it would be impossible to write a "complete" history of the movie theaters of South Carolina. Hopefully, our readers will enjoy what we have included and forgive us for what we have left out.

THE OPERA HOUSE

In the late 1800s, railroads criss-crossed South Carolina transporting farm products to larger markets in the northeast. Lumber, tobacco and cotton were the major crops. These same railroads caused towns to grow along its routes. Many towns built Opera Houses. They served a variety of functions, hosting community dances, fairs, plays, and vaudeville shows as well as operas and other musical events. The railroads brought traveling shows.

To give you an idea of the importance and abundance of Opera Houses in South Carolina, *The Cahn-Leighton Official Theatrical Guide* of 1913, lists twenty-three cities and towns across the state having Opera Houses. The same directory lists another eighteen grand theaters with other names such as Academy of Music or Town Auditorium, which were similar in use and appearance.

Often built as the architectural centerpiece of the town, these Opera Houses were large and imposing. Many of them had the auditorium on the second floor, with the police and fire departments on the ground floor. Towns justified the large expense by making the building a multi-use facility.

Most of these grand theaters had a similar history of presenting live shows, making the transition to silent films and vaudeville, and finally, becoming a movie theater.

Bishopbille, Camden, Clio and Blacksburg had Opera Houses. One of the most beautiful Opera Houses was Charleston's Academy of Music. Greenville, Marion and Laurens had Opera Houses. Most of these magnificent structures are gone, but the beautiful Newberry Opera House and Abbeville's Grand Opera House are still in use.

Newberry Opera House
Still in use.

Newberry Opera House

Construction of the Newberry Opera House was completed in 1881. Built of brick from local brickyards, the French Gothic style building had two floors and a 130-foot clock tower.

The first floor originally housed the fire engine room, city council chambers, a clerk's office, a police office, and three jail cells. The second floor was a performance hall. Some of the acts that performed there included touring companies of New York plays, minstrel and variety shows, famed vocalists and lecturers, magicians and mind readers, novelty acts and boxing exhibitions.

Silent films were shown at the Opera House in the early 1900's. A "talkie" shown in the late teens signaled a change in the use of the house as movies replaced live shows. In the 1930's the Opera House was remodeled as a movie theatre.

The Opera House closed as a movie theatre in 1952. By 1959, the building was in danger of being torn down. In 1970, the building was placed on the National Register of Historic Places.

In 1992 the Newberry Opera House Foundation was formed. Over the next several years, the exterior was restored and an additional 10,000 square feet was added to the building, creating a full theatrical production facility.

Abbeville Opera House
Still in use.

Abbeville Opera House

The day we visited the Abbeville Opera House, we met Michael Genevie, the Executive Director, and Henry Pettit, the Technical Director. For the next several minutes we discussed the theater like old friends comparing common memories. Then, Michael had to attend to some business and we wandered backstage with Henry.

As we looked three stories up at the long ropes holding pieces of scenery, Henry told us about the old theater. "There were touring shows coming out of New York and traveling through here on the way to Atlanta. They stayed overnight at the old Eureka Hotel, which is now the Belmont Inn. Some folks in the community decided that if they built a theater, the touring companies would perform here. The theater opened in 1908."

"They did *Ben Hur* here around 1910 or 1915. There was a cage backstage for the animals. They used the mules to pull the scenery up the ramp and also used them in the show." He told us, "Jimmy Durante, Sarah Bernhardt and Fanny Brice performed here."

"In an old hemp house like this theater," he explained, "the scenery was made of canvas and everything was flown in and out by these ropes. Many of the early stage riggers had been sailors. They communicated from high up there at the pin rail to the stage manager down here by way of different whistles. If you whistled, the stagehand might think he should lower the scenery. That could be fatal to an actor. That's why one should never whistle in a theater."

He opened the large door where the scenery was loaded in and out. It was then that he pointed out the thick back wall of the theater and told us it was the largest free-standing unsupported brick and morter wall in the northern hemisphere. "It hasn't moved in nearly 100 years."

From backstage, Henry took us on a walk through the opera house. We moved through the auditorium to an elevator which took us to the third balcony. We moved cautiously out into the dark balcony which is not currently used. The view of the stage from here is very limited.

Most of the seats were gone. Henry pointed out one single seat at the center of the back row. It was the only complete seat in the row. "That's the ghost's seat." he explained, "There is a ghost in this theater."

Henry took us down the stairs to the first balcony. From here the view was excellent. The curve of the horseshoe balcony framed the stage. The view reenforceed our first impression, that the Abbeville Opera House is a work of art.

Around 1910 many theaters began showing silent films along with their programs of live entertainment. As vaudeville faded, many of these theaters began to show motion pictures exclusively. This was the case with the Abbeville Opera House.

Early movies were often accompanied by live orchestras and sound effects men. When *The Jazz Singer* was released, theaters began to convert to "talkies" or sound films. So did the Abbeville Opera House. By the late 1950's, movie attendance had declined and the Abbeville Opera House closed.

The Abbeville Community Theatre campaigned to save the opera house and in 1978, a summer theatrical season began. A professional touring theater company established residence at the Opera House for the first time since 1917. Currently, with summer and winter theatrical seasons, the Opera House produces 36 weeks of live theater each year.

Auditorium of Abbeville Opera House

Auditorium of Abbeville Opera House

Largest free-standing unsupported brick and morter wall in the northern hemisphere.

Charleston's Academy of Music

The Academy of Music at 225 King Street in Charleston, opened on December 1, 1869. It had the richest history of any theater in the city and was the first theater in Charleston to exhibit films.

The horseshoe shaped auditorium had double tiered galleries supported by iron columns painted gold and white, representing the South Carolina palmetto tree. The ceiling was domed and painted to depict a sky of stars surrounding a "sun burner." This "sun burner" was a large gas lighting fixture containing more than 100 jets of gas flame.

An article in the *News and Courier* from 1896, states that the Academy of Music featured the "Cinematoscope" during a Christmas afternoon matinee. This may have been the first theatrical exhibition of movies in Charleston.

Over the next few years, more movies were shown at the Academy of Music. They were novelties at first, but eventually feature films were shown. An article in the newspaper announced on April 1, 1916, that Lillian Gish, star of *Birth of a Nation* would appear in a film entitled, *The Lilly and the Rose.* The feature would be accompanied by a Keystone Comedy, *The Great Vacuum Robbery,* a parody of *The Great Train Robbery.*

Mr. J. Frampton Baldwin, who worked as a projectionist in Charleston movie theaters for many years, recalled attending the Academy when he was very young. "When I went to the Academy, it was getting very old. They warned us before every show not to stomp our feet or applaud too loudly, as the ceiling plaster would fall."

In the early 1930's, efforts were made to strengthen the deteriorating structure. Engineers made surveys of the building to determine its safety. They strongly recommended that it be torn down.

Academy of Music in Charleston
Closed in 1931 - Torn Down in 1937.

Academy of Music interior

On December 21, 1936, demolition of the Academy of Music began. In 1937 a new theater, the Riviera Theater, was under construction on the site.

Bennettsville's Opera House

The Opera House in Bennettsville is still in use. It went through several renovations and names over the years. It was the Playhouse Theater, Gloria Theater, Carolina Theater, Cinema, and finally the Marlboro Civic Center.

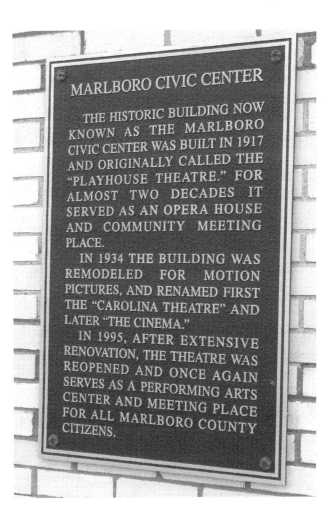

MARLBORO CIVIC CENTER

THE HISTORIC BUILDING NOW KNOWN AS THE MARLBORO CIVIC CENTER WAS BUILT IN 1917 AND ORIGINALLY CALLED THE "PLAYHOUSE THEATRE." FOR ALMOST TWO DECADES IT SERVED AS AN OPERA HOUSE AND COMMUNITY MEETING PLACE.

IN 1934 THE BUILDING WAS REMODELED FOR MOTION PICTURES, AND RENAMED FIRST THE "CAROLINA THEATRE" AND LATER "THE CINEMA."

IN 1995, AFTER EXTENSIVE RENOVATION, THE THEATRE WAS REOPENED AND ONCE AGAIN SERVES AS A PERFORMING ARTS CENTER AND MEETING PLACE FOR ALL MARLBORO COUNTY CITIZENS.

Playhouse Theater (1920s)

Cinema (1980s)

Marlboro Civic Center (2008)

In the early 1900s, adventurous businessmen opened arcades, also known as Nickelodeons. They were filled with viewing machines. These early machines, known by various names such as Kinetoscope or Mutoscop, allowed one person at a time to look into a box and view a film, usually for the price of a nickel.

One way to understand the popularity of the Kinetoscope is to hear the story of Mr. Egbert A. Armistead's experience with them in his notions store around 1905. His grandson, John A. Armistead, of Easley, shared this story with us.

The Armistead family entry into motion picture exhibiting

By John Anderson Armistead

Egbert's insightful good humor, his energy and enthusiasm, as well as his gentlemanly ways made his notions business a success. One day a salesman in a wagon came in. Egbert asked, "How may I help you, Sir?"

"Oh, I'm not here to buy. I'm here to interest you in a money making opportunity!" The salesman proceded to describe the kinetoscope to Egbert. "I'll give you a free demonstration. I'll even give the first ten customers a nickel so that they can see it and get the word out! How does that sound?"

Soon the tall machine was standing upright in a vacant part of the floor near the front window. The movie machine salesman said, "Isn't it a work of art?" A small crowd gathered outside, looking at the brightly painted red and gold case, and the carved cherubs around the top, like on a calliope.

Egbert Anderson Armistead, Sr.

"She's all ready, Egbert. Look through here and I'll drop in a nickel for you." Egbert looked into the kinetoscope. "Wow! This is a much better picture than flip books have. That boy is running without hardly a flicker! You can even see the water splashing up when he jumps in the pond. And there are *girls* wading in the pond. *Cute*, too!

Word of the kinetoscope spread quickly. As stores around town closed, there were people still lined up for their chance to see the new movie machine. Egbert counted the number of clicks he heard of nickels dropping in. The next day, a crowd of people lined up all afternoon to see it, for a nickel each.

Soon there were two kinetoscope machines in the store, then there were three, then four. There weren't enough hours in the day for everyone to watch. People got tired of standing waiting in line. But, having people standing in line brought in more business than ever before. "This is the best thing I've had in here since I rented a cotton candy machine." said Egbert.

Soon, the movie machine salesman returned and told Egbert, "Edison is coming out with rolls of film played on a big projector. It flashes pictures on a screen so several people can see the same film at the same time. Would you be interested in going into the movie business full time? Other companies are beginning to turn out moving pictures faster and better than the Edison folks. I'm going to be distributing every new film I can get my hands on. Will you commit to putting in a screen and buying a projector?"

Egbert replied, "I like the idea of being able to show films when I want to show them, not just when people happen by. Keeping these nickel machines running requires me to work too many hours. But I like the money we make." So began the Armistead family in the motion picture business.

SILENT MOVIES - NOT TRUE!

We can hear music anywhere and anytime we want. When the movies first appeared, the only music one could hear was by live performers. Recorded music and radio were not widely available.

The earliest film arcades and theaters provided color slide shows along with motion pictures. These slide shows, called "Illustrated Songs," were accompanied by a pianist and singer who sometimes encouraged the audience to sing along. The short films of the time were only part of a program of entertainment.

As the movie became the only entertainment shown, they were accompanied by a piano or organ. In larger movie theaters, small orchestras or pit bands provided music to add the right emotional environment for the action on screen.

Mildred Higgins recalled seeing movies at the Princess Theater in Georgetown in the late 1920s. She said they had a player piano. She explained that it sometimes made them laugh because the music on the paper piano rolls didn't always match the action on the screen. "Fast music might come out of the piano during a love scene, or something slow and sad might be playing during a comic scene," she said, "But, we were glad to have it."

The Garden Theater in Charleston had an American Fotoplayer. This was a very special piano built exclusively for movie theaters. It could be played like a regular piano, but it had a separate unit containing sound effects and special instruments which could be played by way of pull-ropes on the console. Mrs. Margaret Dengate played at the Garden Theater between 1918 and 1927. She recalled playing an American Fotoplayer, "I could make the sounds of shooting pistols, slamming doors, creaks and others."

American Fotoplayer

Typical Pit Band in 1920s movie theater
Drummer also provided sound effects

When the Gloria Theater opened in Charleston on August 19, 1927, the crowds enjoyed the new theater organ. The opening film presentation was "After Midnight" starring Norma Shearer. This silent film was accompanied by Mrs. Margaret Dengate on the new organ. When we interviewed Mrs. Dengate in 1992, she said, "I didn't know what was going on in the theatre. I couldn't look at anything. I had to watch the screen.

The Carolina Theater in Greenville had an organ when it opened in 1925. It was a Wurlitzer Opus 1028 E that cost $20,000.

From 1925 Wurlitzer advertisement.
Prices range from $5,000 to $150,000

Records of the Wurlitzer Company state that a Wurlitzer organ was shipped to the Imperial Theater in Columbia on March 14, 1928. Their records also show shipment of organs to the Rex/State Theater in Orangeburg on June 12, 1927. Greenville received organs at the Egyptian Theater and Rivoli Theater. On November 26, 1937 Wurlitzer shipped an organ to the Carolinian Theater in Orangeburg. Smaller Wurlitzer organs were installed in many South Carolina movie theaters, but were probably purchased from smaller distributors.

Many of the theater organs were moved to churches after theaters installed sound equipment in the early 1930s. Some of them were simply broken apart and dumped. In some rare cases these extraordinary instruments have survived in place. The Atlanta Fox has a custome built Moller organ, known as the "Mighty Moe," which can still be heard on special occasions. It is the second largest theater organ in the country, next to the Wurlitzer at Radio City Music Hall in New York City.

None of the organs in South Carolina's theaters were nearly as grand as the ones at the Atlanta Fox or Radio City Music Hall. But, they thrilled audiences with their commanding sounds.

In 1914, the Princess Theatre introduced a five-piece orchestra to accompany the films and entertain with songs between features. The orchestra was under the direction of Theo Wichmann. They began playing every day at 3:30 p.m. and continued until 6:30 when they stopped to eat supper. At 7:30 the orchestra was back and played until the theatre closed.

Charleston's *Evening Post* on January 11, 1924, advertised the film "Broken Wing" at the Charleston Theater, 566 King Street. The Ammes Orchestra played during the film at the ususal hours and prices.

Thematic cue sheets were frequently provided to the cinema pianist, either by the movie studio, which distributed these music sheets along with the film, or, by music publishers who provided generic music cue sheets to fit a variety of scenes and moods in the movies.

These movie cue sheets told the pianist what to play and when to play it. They even contained "cues" to tell the pianist when to change the speed and style of music so that it would best relate the feeling of the images on the screen.

Charlie Chaplin composed the music for his outstanding silent film "City Lights." He called the film a "comedy romance" and made it after sound films had become popular. We attended a showing of "City Lights" at Gaillard Auditorium in Charleston in 1996. The Royal Liverpool Philharmonic Orchestra played Chaplin's original movie score, as restored by Carl Davis.

When the movie ended and the orchestra's last note faded away, there was not a sound to be heard. The 2,700 people attending sat in stunned silence at both Chaplin's masterpiece and the breathtaking performance of the symphony orchestra. Then, a light applause grew into a thunderous one as everyone rose to their feet. Such is the power of great film and great music, expecially when that music is performed live.

∫INGLE-∫CREEN MOVIE THEATER∫

In the early 1920s, audiences found a combination of live performances and motion pictures at their local theaters. After the decline of touring shows and vaudeville, these theaters often became full-time movie houses. As the popularity of movies grew, theaters were built for the single purpose of exhibiting films.

South Carolina's single-screen movie theaters took many forms, from simple wood-frame buildings seating 100 people or less, to large attractive brick structures with over 1,000 seats.

We present a representative account of those theaters. But, the real story of the movie theaters in South Carolina is found in the memories of the people who ran them and those who attended them regularly. Before we get to the theaters, we offer some special memories from Mrs. Emily Padgett and her family to provide context and perspective.

Left to Right: Gayle McCullough, Emily Padgett and Thad McCullough

Five Generations Go to the Movies

Mrs. Emily Padgett was born in Fort Mill, South Carolina in 1914. In an interview on September 2, 2005, she shared her memories of going to the movies with her father in Fort Mill. Her daughter, Gayle McCullough, and Gayle's husband, Thad, shared their movie-going memories too.

Mrs. Emily Padgett:
I saw my first picture show at the Majestic Theatre in Fort Mill, South Carolina. We lived about two blocks from the theatre. The theatre was owned by Mr. Bradford. His daughter was a good friend of mine. Her aunt was the woman behind the counter where you bought your tickets. Tickets were ten cents for children and a quarter for adults.

All we had was music with the movie, you know. It was before "talkies." I think it was a record or something. I don't remember how they played the music.

My father [Sam Meacham] owned the electric company in Fort Mill. He wired all the houses and put in the telephones. He owned the telephone company too. His office was around the corner from the theatre. The back door to his office was right across from the back door of the movie house. So, whenever anything went wrong with the projector, they would come and get Papa.

Samuel Lewis Meacham

Because he did that, they let us [his children] in free. He didn't charge them anything, so we could get in free anytime we wanted to. They only had movies on Friday and Saturday. On Friday, they ran from 6 o'clock to 9, and on Saturday, from 1 o'clock to 9. In a small town, there was not much to do after 9 p.m.

My mother didn't care for picture shows. My father took my sister and me. My mother stayed home with the baby boy. She would let us go with my father but we couldn't go by ourselves.

We would go every Friday and Saturday but we had to wait until he could leave his office and take us. On Saturday afternoons from 1 o'clock on, we kept listening for him. My sister and I wanted to get there to see the serials. They had a serial every Friday and Saturday, a different one. So, that was two serials you had to keep up with. They would have short comedies and news and other things, too.

Mostly, they showed Westerns. These were silent picture shows so you had to read what people said. Papa would read aloud what everybody was saying. He would read them to us and after awhile, we'd look around, and there would be four or five other children gathered around there listening to him.

We would be watching a movie and the picture would go out. Papa would tell everybody to wait. He would go fix it and then come and sit back down.

One of my uncles [John Alexander Boyd, Jr.] laughed really loud when he got tickled. He laughed so loud that they let him in free when there was a funny movie. He made everybody else laugh, too. Anybody outside could hear him so they would pay to come in and see what was so funny. This increased business for the theatre.

We knew who all the movie stars were. My sister and I would play like we were one of them. At home we would act out things. She would pretend to be one actress and I would play another.

Gayle McCullough:
My daddy was sick for a couple of years and my brother, mother and I lived with Mama's parents. We would go to the movies every Saturday afternoon in the same theatre Mama frequented when she was a child. We saw the serial and cartoons, previews, and two Westerns. And it lasted all afternoon.

Mama would give us a quarter apiece. It cost nine cents to get in. The popcorn cost five cents and the drink cost six cents. That added up to twenty cents which left us a nickel to buy ice cream on the way home.

At that time, during World War II, Mama would let my brother and me walk to the theatre alone. I was about six and my brother, Duncan, was four. They had a ticket box-office by then. They did have a marquee then and posters. Everyone in town knew us and it was quite safe.

One Saturday, for some reason, the movie didn't start at 1 o'clock. It started at 3 o'clock. We didn't know any better so we waited in line. All the children waited in line. We were supposed to have been home about 5 o'clock, but because it started late, we were still there watching the movie. All of a sudden Papa came in and told us to get ourselves home! I guess he thought we were watching the movie a second time.

That scared us to death. We didn't understand why he seemed so mad at us. I remember crying all the way home. I think Papa felt really bad when he realized what had happened.

My grandfather became interested in the new invention, the telephone, when he was a young boy. Papa's father had been a doctor and owned a pharmacy. Sometimes he would be at the drugstore and sometimes at the house. If somebody came to the house and needed the doctor and he was at the drugstore, Papa's mother would make Papa run to the drugstore and get his daddy. After awhile, Papa got tired of running back and forth between his home and the pharmacy. He had heard about a new invention called the telephone. So, he rigged up phones between the pharmacy and the house.

It has been said that Mr. Springs, who owned the mill, heard about the doctor's phone and wanted one put in between his home and the main office at the mill. Papa borrowed enough money to buy eight telephones to set up in Fort Mill. He also set up the first phones in Pineville, North Carolina. He set up the electricity in Fort Mill and Pineville too.

Mrs. Emily Padgett:
People would always call the operator to find out where anybody was. She kept up with everybody. When there was a fire, Papa would call the operator to find out where it was. Then, he would rush over to take out his electric meter so it wouldn't be destroyed. Sometimes he would beat the firemen and they always wanted to know how he knew where the fire was.

Thad McCullough:
I grew up in Columbia. They had the Carolina, Palmetto, Ritz, Strand and the State all on Main Street. Every Saturday morning a bunch of the neighborhood kids would get together and we would go to the movies. The Ritz Theatre was the most popular because they showed Westerns.

One of the popular Western stars was Lash LaRue. His sidekick was Fuzzy St. John, who was a bearded fellow with a floppy hat. He wore his pistols criss-crossed in his belt. He stood on the stage at the Ritz Theatre, which was packed with young children. He was telling jokes. Then he was telling about running away from this bad man when he stopped and turned around. Then he reached down for his two pistols and fired blanks. The children started to scream and run out of the theatre. I'll never forget that. My brother wet his britches.

Another time we went over to the Strand across the street. They were having a Western we wanted to see. One of my good friends, Walter, who lived in back of us, my brother and another boy and I were sitting eating popcorn. The theatre was packed. A lady brought her children and sat right in front of us. All of a sudden, Walter got sick and threw up all over this lady.

I sent my brother to tell the movie theatre people that our friend spit up all over this woman. They stopped the movie and turned the lights on and came to help her out. She was covered with it. He couldn't help it. To this day when I see him I ask him if he remembers the Strand Theatre and he says, "Don't remind me!"

When we visited in Kingstree, my Aunt Dorothy took my two brothers and me to the Anderson Theatre one evening to see a movie with Barbara Stanwyck. I forget the name of it. At that age I wasn't really into Barbara Stanwyck. I got so bored I got up and went outside. I walked all around downtown Kingstree. My aunt thought I had gone to the restroom. When I finally came back and sat down, the movie was almost over.

My aunt said, "What happened? Did you get sick?" I said, "No ma'am. I just walked around town." She got very upset. "You mean you walked around town by yourself at night?" I never thought anything about it.

Gayle McCullough:
After World War II, between 1946 and 1951, we lived in Shandon on Heyward Street. My friends and I went to nearly every movie that came to the theatres. When I was eight or nine years old, we could go downtown by ourselves. There was a bus stop right on the corner near our house. We would get on the bus and go downtown. Then, we had only one block to walk to Main Street.

The Carolina Theatre was the one closest to the State House, then the Ritz and the Palmetto. The State and the Strand were across the street. My group of friends thought the side with the State and the Strand was the rough side of the street. I don't think I ever went to a movie on that side of the street.

Many times we would go to the movie at the Carolina and then to the Ritz and then to the Palmetto. We spent the whole day watching movies. Then we would walk to Sumter Street and catch the bus and go home.

I kept up with the movie stars back then. I mean, I knew everybody who was married to everybody or was dating anybody. I bought every movie magazine and cut out the pictures and made a scrapbook. I remember parting with that scrapbook one Christmas. We had a cousin, Caroline, who loved movies. She had suffered some brain damage in an accident when she was a young child. I just decided to give her my scrapbook for Christmas and she loved it.

My brother remembers getting into the movie in Columbia for bringing a mashed-up tin can. This would have been 1946, just after the war. He couldn't figure out why they were still collecting metal but I guess the metal had all been used up in the war.

I wanted to talk about the theatre in Five Points [in Columbia] because that's where I would go on Saturdays. The Five Points Theatre was within walking distance of our house on Heyward Street. They would have people on stage entertaining the children before the movie, which would be a children's movie. I think we paid ten cents to get in.

Either my mother or my aunt would take us and drop us off for the morning. My aunt lived about two blocks away from us. My cousin, her only child, was about four years old and I was eleven or twelve. One time they took my little cousin and me to see "The Wizard of Oz." The tornado scene, which comes very early in the movie, scared him to death! He started screaming and crying. I had to take him to the theatre office and call my aunt. I had to wait a long time while my aunt walked from her house, down Harden Street to the theatre. I missed half of the movie and was very perturbed but I do understand how that scene could frighten a young child.

When Thad and I first met, we usually went to movies on our dates. My favorite movie was "The Prince Who Was a Thief" I think that starred Tony Curtis and Piper Laurie. It was set back in the time of the sheiks. I thought it was wonderful and I saw it seven times.

As a young person, I loved "Broken Arrow" too, but that was because it starred Debra Paget. My name was Padgett. She spelled her name differently. I even wrote her saying "Maybe we're kin to each other." You know how children are. I thought she must be my cousin or something. She sent me her picture with an autograph. I later found out her real name was Debralee Griffin!

Debra Padget

When we moved to Sullivan's Island in 1951, the Fort Theatre was an old dilapidated place. I do remember taking our two oldest children there when they had a children's movie one night. I think they only opened on weekends occasionally but I always wished someone would take it over and open it at least during the summer months.

You asked if we ever sneaked into the movies. No, we didn't. However, you were not supposed to bring refreshments into the theater. I had four small children and I would make popcorn before we left home and put it in small plastic bags. I didn't have any drinks but maybe I had candy bars. I put everything in a big pocket book and when we got into the movie I would hand out all of it. That's kind of like sneaking into the movies I guess.

As a high school student, I went to the Parkway Theatre [in Mount Pleasant] nearly every weekend. Mr. Query did the concessions. After the theatre closed it was the Krispy Kreme shop. Then, the Krispy Kreme moved down to the corner.

At this time Gayle and Thad's son, Joel, came in with Joel's son, Bryce. Bryce climbed onto Gayle's lap. Joel recalled his movie-going experiences while attending Baptist College. He remembered going to the Fox Theatre in Gaslight Square [North Charleston] because they only charged one dollar. As a college student, that was all he could afford. Gayle asked her grandson if he remembered the first movie she took him to see. Bryce said, "Finding Nemo!"

Gayle:
Well, that's five generations of going to the movies in South Carolina. Mama's daddy took her to see her first movie at the Majestic Theatre in Fort Mill. I took my grandson, Bryce, to see his first movie at the Palmetto Grand in Mount Pleasant.

Aiken

Aiken Grand Opera House, on Park Street, is listed in 1913 *Julius Cahn and Gus Hill Theatrical Guide and Moving Picture Directory*. The Princess Theatre is listed in the 1921 edition of the directory. The guide lists Aiken's population in 1921 at 4,103.

In 1922, Mr. J.H. Welborn leased the Opera House and opened it as the Aiken Theater.

The Augusta Chronicle - March 8, 1922

It is said that nothing but high class motion pictures will be shown at the theatre, and the management has promised to secure the same photoplays as shown in Augusta.

One problem with the Aiken Theater was that it shared the building with the local fire department.

The Augusta Chronicle – May 31, 1925

What came very nearly being a frightful catastrophe was only narrowly averted by the cool action of a few at the Aiken Theatre last night during the commencement exercises of the Aiken Institute. Contrary to the judgment of many, the Aiken Fire Department is located under the theatre, and at the alarm of fire last night, when White Hall, a winter home was ablaze, the alarm sounding right in the ears of the packed audience, created a panic at once. Nearly every one in the audience jumped to his feet, and several leaped from the lower windows, while many rushed to reach the main entrance amid the cries and shouts of children and guardians.

Apparently, this incident didn't panic anyone enough to move the fire department. In 1927 Aiken patrons were thrilled to see the famous comedian Will Rogers. Many from Augusta also attended.

The Augusta Chronicle
February 15, 1927

The appearance of Will Rogers, the American comedian, was a splendid success Sunday evening at the Aiken Theatre, a two-thousand-five-hundred-dollar house greeting the famous humorist. In the audience were many of the New York, Boston, Philadelphia and Chicago elite, and perhaps no entertainment in Aiken has ever attracted a larger number of Augustans than did that of Rogers. The humorist was presented to the audience by Herbert E. Gyles, who, in the midst of his praise of Rogers was stopped by the humorist, who poked his head from behind the screen and shouted, "That's enough of that!"

The first talking pictures were exhibited at the Aiken Theater in 1928.

The Augusta Chronicle – March 22, 1928

Talking motion pictures will be shown at the Aiken Theatre tonight only, starting at 9:00 o'clock, and an elaborate program of these wonder films produced by the Fox Film Corp., is announced in the advertising columns of today's *Chronicle*. These talking pictures are known as "Movietone Pictures" and are said to be very realistic and lifelike.

It is also stated that Wm. Fox well known movie producer and President of the Fox Film Corporation will be present in person at the premier showing of the talking pictures.

In 1932, the Aiken Theater was renamed the State Theater, under the management of Mr. H.B. Ram.

The Augusta Chronicle
January 29, 1932

The Aiken Theatre, renamed State Theatre, will definitely open Wednesday, H.R. Ram, manager, stated this week. Mr. Ram had hoped to begin his shows this weekend, but was inadvertently prevented from so doing.

By 1936, Mr. Ram had decided to build a new motion picture theater. His plans were announced in the *Augusta Chronicle* of December 11, 1936. Plans called for the new theater to be located on the site of the "Loomis residence" on Laurens Street.

These plans turned out to be a very good idea. On August 11, 1938, shortly before the new theater was finished, fire broke out in the projection room of the State Theater and quickly spread.

The Augusta Chronicle
August 17, 1938

The fire, which caught about 8 o'clock Thursday night in the projection room of the State Theatre quickly spread until in a short while the whole building was engulfed in flames. All that was left of the building were the brick walls.

Mr. Ram announced that an extra force would be put to work on the erection of his new theater building on Laurens Street and in about two months he hoped to have the building ready for use.

The Patricia Theater built by Mr. Ram in the 900 block of Laurens Street, opened October 7, 1938.

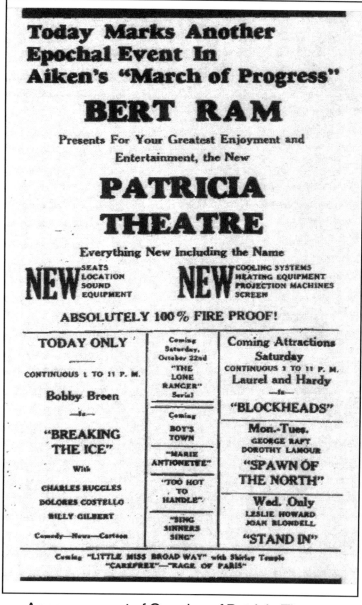

Announcement of Opening of Patricia Theater on October 7, 1938

He named the theater for his daughter Patricia Ram. Pat Ram Fawilowsky, who now lives in Pembroke Pines, Fla., recalled leaving the Patricia Theater in December, 1941. "I remember walking home from there, and Pearl Harbor had just been bombed," she said.

Patricia Theater in 1955

Mr. Ram opened the Rosemary Theater, named for another daughter, on February 14, 1950 in the same block of Laurens Street as the Patricia Theater.

The Rosemary Theater had a history similar to most other local movie houses in the 1950s. On one occasion, in 1950, the Jaycees sponsored a cartoon show for local children.

An hour and a half of cartoons were offered. The only admission price was three soap wrappers from bars of Swan soap. This benefitted the CARE organization.

In 1951, Mr. Ram renovated the Rosemary Theater increasing its seating from 700 seats to 1,000 seats. He also added a smoking loge in the first balcony, added a new "Typhoon" air-conditioning plant, and made other improvements.

In 1955, Mr. Cecil Farr managed both the Patricia and Rosemary Theaters. A newspaper article that year described his typical Saturday at the theaters.

"Every Saturday he shepherds 300 to 400 youngsters through the adventures of "Jungle Jim" and "The Man from Outer Space" or some other hair-raising double feature – plus a serial which leaves the hero dangling in mid-air, clutching the edge of a cliff with weakening finger tips.

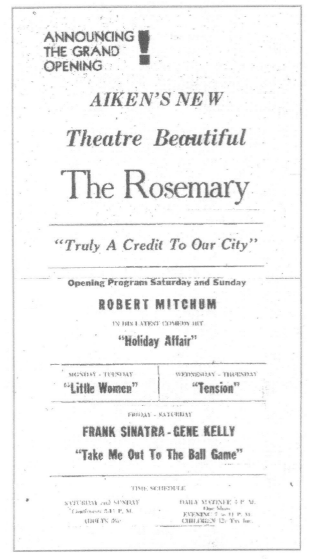

ANNOUNCING THE GRAND OPENING!

AIKEN'S NEW

Theatre Beautiful

The Rosemary

"Truly A Credit To Our City"

Opening Program Saturday and Sunday

ROBERT MITCHUM

IN HIS LATEST COMEDY HIT

"Holiday Affair"

MONDAY - TUESDAY	WEDNESDAY - THURSDAY
"Little Women"	"Tension"

FRIDAY - SATURDAY

FRANK SINATRA - GENE KELLY

"Take Me Out To The Ball Game"

TIME SCHEDULE

February 14, 1950

During the afternoon at least a dozen youngsters have lost one of the following articles; a wallet containing a nickel, a super-sonic ray gun, a shirt taken off in the heat of excitement, a package of bubble gum, or a pair of shoes.

He is assisted by W.E. Shuler, the quiet, gray-haired gentleman who is usually in the lobby of the Rosemary Theater. Mr. Shuler knows all his patrons, big and little, and gives them a friendly nod as they go in.

In a small city such as Aiken, theaters are a community institution. Films are carefully selected for family entertainment, and youngsters are kept under a watchful eye. Mr. Farr and Mr. Shuler make a tour of the houses every half hour, and on Saturdays two ushers are in constant attendance at both theaters."

Both the Rosemary Theater and Patricia Theater were leased by Stewart & Everett. The Patricia Theater closed in 1961 and ceased operation as a movie theater. In 1963 Stewart & Everett made major renovations to the Rosemary Theater and renamed it the Cinema. Over the next several years it had a second screen added, and then a third, becoming the Cinema Triplex.

In 1987 Carmike Cinemas took over operation of the theater. It closed the Cinema Triplex on April 5, 2001, as its parent company struggled through bankruptcy proceedings.

"It's going to affect downtown Aiken in a major way" said Lisa Revels, theater manager.

"Luckily, I've found another job," added assistant manager Katie Brummel.

Most of the staff members were teen-agers. One employee said the idea of converting the downtown site into a "dollar theater" (showing movies at cut rates) deserved exploration, and added, "They could have explored other avenues."

The Carmike facility had been Aiken's only downtown cinema since the closure and demolition of Mark Twin, on Newberry Street, in 1999.

Mr. H.B. (Bert) Ram

Mr. Ram, a native of Stanford, Connecticut, came to Aiken because of the mildness of the local climate. He was with the Paramount distributing company for many years and was trained in the fundamentals of the motion picture distribution and operation.

He left Paramount in the late 1920s to manage the Ithaca, New York theaters. In 1930 he came to Aiken and took over the old State Theater, which was located on Park Avenue on the site of the present Municipal building.

Later he purchased the Carolina Theater in Batesburg, and when the State Theater burned in 1938, he built and opened the Patricia Theater and developed the portion of the block on Laurens Street which housed his two theaters, the Rosemary and the Patricia. After building the first of those theaters he expanded his civic development and owned a number of store houses on Laurens Street.

Mr. Ram died in 1970.

ANDERSON

The Anderson Theater was located at 204 West Whitner Street from 1915 to 1924. The Gloria Theater operated at this location from 1924 until 1931. On May 29, 1931 the Criterion Theater opened on this site.

The Criterion Theater was a beautiful movie house. According to Jim Compton, who was Assistant Manager of the theater from 1947 to 1950, it was very ornate in its construction. It featured a large marble lobby. It had 500 seats on the main level, 150 seats in the balcony and six box seats on either side near the large stage.

Mr. Compton recalled that, during the late 1940s into the early 1950s, lines for tickets stretched clear around the block on Thursday, Friday and Saturday nights. The Criterion closed in 1960 and has been demolished.

Criterion Theater interior
during demolition in 1967

Photographs of the Criterion Theatre, courtesy
Pendleton District Commission, Pendleton, SC

The Strand Theatre opened in 1920, at 126 N. Main Street. It showed the first talking picture in Anderson, "The Lion and the Mouse." In 1946, it became the Center Theatre. The Center Theatre closed in 1955.

Marquee of Strand Theater is visible
in this photo from the 1930s

The Carolina Theatre opened at 201 North Main Street in 1932 and closed in 1957.

Carolina Theater

Six Bottle Caps

The high school football coach in Anderson remembered when admission to a Saturday movie at the State Theater was six Coca-Cola bottle caps He and his buddies would go to the corner grocery store. One would distract the grocer while the others tipped the cap box on the drink machine and collected all the bottle caps in a hat. Outside, they would sort through the caps finding six each of the right brand so they could all get into the movie theater for free.

ACT Theater - Ticket Booth

State Theater (1939-1972)
131 East Whitner Street

ACT Theater - Formerly State Theater

Harry Osteen

Harry Osteen, Sr. was not only a theater owner, but a theater historian. He produced a DVD called, "The History of Theaters in Anderson, S.C." which he narrated. His father, Mr. P.C. Osteen operated several theaters in Anderson that showed motion pictures and staged vaudeville performances. Between 1946 and 1974, Harry, along with his brothers Percy, Bill, and Albert, opened a series of movie theaters in Anderson.

Harry Osteen

BEAUFORT

Photo courtesy Beaufort County Library
Lucille Hassell Culp Collection

The Ritz Theater is the first known movie theater in Beaufort. According to *The Beaufort Gazette* of September 12, 1927, it opened with a packed house. The manager, W.A. Murphy promised that order would prevail during all pictures. Two air cooling machines provided for a pleasant evening, even on the hottest night.

The Breeze Theater opened in 1936 on the corner of Bay and West Streets. We were told the building was a bank that was converted into a movie theater. The columns were removed and dumped into the marsh. When the current owner was remodeling the building as a restaurant, he had the old columns pulled from the marsh, where they had been resting for many years, cleaned and replaced as they had been when the building was a bank.

The Palm Theater opened in Beaufort around 1947. It didn't have a long existence as it was closed about ten years later. At that time there were two drive-ins operating in the Beaufort area; the Greenlawn Drive-In and the Royal Drive-In.

All of these theaters are now gone, including the drive-ins. However, Beaufort has one of the few remaining drive-ins still in operation. The Highway 21 Drive-In offers a fun family outing to local residents and the curious from far away.

Former bank building and Breeze Theater this location is now a restaurant.

BISHOPVILLE

"When this building came available, The Chamber of Commerce bought it. We've looked over hell and half of Georgia trying to come up with a good community bulletin board that fits the character of the downtown. We didn't want one of those signs you put on the sidewalk. We rebuilt the theater marquee and now we change the letters when we have an event. We've gotten lots of compliments on it.

RE—OPENS This Week

The Harper Theater, formerly the Andrews, opened in 1983. It closed after one month.

When we arrived in Bishopville, we saw that the Visitor Center had an old movie theater marquee. Ronnie Williams, Executive Director of the Lee County Chamber of Commerce, explained that the building had been the Andrews Theater.

He took us up to the balcony level and down a short hall. He said, "This used to be the theater manager's office." The office was bright with windows opening to the street.

We followed him up to the projection booth. In the dust and debris stood two carbon arc lamps. They were used to focus light through the projectors onto the screen. On a shelf near the door were old reels of movie film.

Ronnie told us "A fellow from Hartsville came over here and reopened the theater as the Harper Theater in 1983, but it didn't stay open a month. It didn't have the traffic to keep it going."

Ronnie Williams in the projection booth

BELTON

Belton had two theaters listed in the *Film Daily Yearbook* of 1945, the Belton and the Virginia. On a visit to Belton in 2003, we learned of another theatre called the Joy.

Very often the local movie theater had a barber shop in or next to the theater building. We stopped in the barber shop and met Homer Booth. He was busy with a customer. He paused while we introduced ourselves and explained what we were trying to find. "It was right next door where The Jean Shop is now," he said. "Go ask Eunice Fields to show you. You can still see some of it upstairs."

At The Jean Shop, Mrs. Fields listened as we explained our mission. "It's really dark up there but I'll be glad to take you," she said. A friend said she would get a flashlight.

At the back of the store, the four of us cautiously climbed the old creaking stairs. We came to a door and beyond it were more dark stairs. As we came to the top of the stairs and turned we found ourselves in a huge room. It had six hanging lights and could have been a ballroom. On the street side of the building we entered two smaller rooms that had fire places and windows overlooking Main Street. "Keep going," Mrs. Fields said. "Open that door there on your right."

We opened the door and saw what remained of the Belton Theater. It was the balcony, or at least a part of the balcony. Beyond the railing it was very dark. The flashlight revealed risers where the balcony seats had once been. Renovations to the building had been made to accommodate the new businesses. It was impossible to determine how large the Belton Theater had been or to know what it had looked like in its active years. But, we still had an exciting sense of discovery.

When we were back downstairs, Mrs. Fields suggested we talk to the pharmacist, Mr. Henry Clinkscales. We were glad to go into the corner drug store and get out of the summer heat. Mr. Clinkscales listened graciously to our story and smiled as we described the balcony of the Belton Theater we had just seen above The Jeans Store. We asked if he had been to the Belton Theater.

Henry Clinkscales

June 26, 2003

Oh Lord, yes! Every Saturday afternoon. There were three movie theaters in Belton and Mr. Adger Gray owned all of them. The Belton Theater was originally an old Opera House. You'll notice it's in the only three-story building in town. The marquee used to hang out over the sidewalk. Mr. Gray bought it in the late 1920s or early 1930s. Then, during the war, there were three buildings where the bank parking lot is now. One was a restaurant, one was the Virginia Theater and the other was a Dodge dealership.

Right at the end of the square they built the Joy Theater. That was about 1947 or 1948. It was supposed to be state-of-the-art. There was a room for crying babies. It had a wonderful snack room and was famous for the hot dogs. Sometimes movie stars came to town to promote their films.

When I was twelve or thirteen, Lash LaRue came to town. He rode his horse right down the aisle of the theater. He did whip tricks. He would get someone to hold a cigarette in their mouth and he'd cut it down with his whip. Then, if you bought a picture of him for fifty cents, he would autograph it. I didn't have fifty cents so I tore a popcorn box and he signed it. Gabby Hayes was here too.

On Monday and Tuesday was one movie. Then, on Wednesday, was a different movie, usually a "B" movie with short subjects. The movie changed again for Thursday and Friday. Then on Saturday they always showed a western with a cartoon and maybe The Three Stooges. That would show until about ten o'clock.

This drugstore has been in my family since 1895. When I was in high school I worked here behind the soda fountain. All my friends would come by when the drugstore closed and we would go to the late show on Saturday night. It started a little after ten o'clock and was usually a scary movie and a serial. We had to be home by twelve.

I remember my dad asking me to go to the bank up the street about three blocks to get him some change. The World Series was on the radio. This was long before people had air conditioning and all the shops had their doors open. As I walked up the street I could hear the series from every store. I walked the three blocks up and back and didn't miss any of the game.

"The Belton Theater was originally an old Opera House. You'll notice it's in the only three-story building in town."

Polio Scare Closes Theaters

Palmetto Theater - Columbia
August, 1939 - Polio Ban Lifted

Columbia Schools to Close Today

Columbia, S.C. May 23, 1939
With total infantile paralysis cases in the state reported at 119 since November, the Columbia City schools prepared today to close their classes ahead of schedule as a precautionary measure against any outbreak of the disease here.

Ban Lifted

Greenville, S.C. August 14, 1939
Health authorities lifted today the ban on gatherings of children under 12 years of age in Greenville County. It was imposed several weeks ago as a precaution to stop spread of infantile paralyses.

CAMDEN

Mr. T. Lee Little opened the Majestic Theater at 506 Dekalb Street in Camden on April 7, 1915. The opening attraction was "Wildflower" starring Marguerite Clark and Harlold Lockwood. Mr. Little brought the Mac Sennett bathing beauties to appear in person at the Majestic Theater. This was the first time citizens of Camden saw the new form-fitting bathing suits that had become the national rage. One episode of the movie serial, "Perils of Pauline" was filmed in Camden. In April, 1950, the Majestic Theater became the Little Theater.

The Haigler Theater, also known as the King Haigler Theater, was located on the southeast corner of the intersection of Broad and Rutledge Streets, the site of the former Opera House. The Haigler Theater was named for Catawba Chief King Haigler, the beloved chief of the Catawbas, who befriended early settlers in the Camden area.

The Camden Theater was another movie theater opened by Mr. T. Lee Little.

Our gratitude to Gretchen Roepke, granddaughter of Mr. T. Lee Little for providing most of this information.

In the 1900's, before getting into motion picture exhibition, Mr. T. Lee Little brought fair attractions and carnivals to Camden. He booked "live" shows into the Opera House. He booked the motion picture "Birth of a Nation" into the Opera House as a special attraction with accompaniment of a full orchestra.

One of the South's pioneer exhibitors, Mr. Little began operating his Majestic Theater in Camden on April 7, 1915. He opened the 1,000-seat Little Theater in 1948 to replace the Majestic. He also operated the Haigler Theater and the Sky-Vue Drive-In.

He was a member of the North Carolina - South Carolina Theater Owners Association and the Camden Executives Club as well as a charter member of the Camden Rotary Club. In 1950, he was honored by Paramount Pictures on his 35th anniversary as an exhibitor of Paramount's films. He received an engraved scroll bearing congratulation and well wishes of Paramount executives, including Adolph Zukor. He also received telegrams from virtually every movie star on the Paramount lot.

T. Lee Little

An artice published in the *Camden Chronicle* in 1955, states, "Few exhibitors can claim such a lengthy career. In the whole of South Carolina, only "old-timers," Lee Little [of Camden] and Albert Sottile of Charleston, have remained independent exhibitors against the inroads of the chains and the ravages of time and fortune."

Little Theater Marquee in the 1960s

Little Theater - Camden

CHARLESTON

Understanding how the movies became what they are today is easy. Understanding how people viewed motion pictures around 1900 is difficult. Looking back to those days is a bit like looking through the wrong end of a telescope. Movies were new. No one knew quite what they were. To most, they were moving photographs or some kind of magic slight of hand. They were amusements, not yet telling stories but rather showing scenes. They were a street scene in New York, a train wreck, or a kiss. These scenes did not justify a venue. They were exhibited in lecture halls or tents. The early films shown in Charleston were outside at Chicora Park after dark or at the local Y.M.C.A. When movies first made their way to a theater, it was Charleston's Academy of Music on the corner of King and Market Streets.

A few adventurous souls, like James Sottile and George and Florence Brantley saw the potential for a profitable business in exhibiting these novelties. They opened small theaters in rented storefronts on King Street. The Brantleys opened the Theatorium at 321 King Street, using a large piece of cheesecloth for a screen and 114 kitchen chairs for seats. James Sottile opened his little storefront theater at 282 King Street and called it the Pastime Theater. Both were very popular and successful enterprises.

E.J. Riddock and William J. Byrnes soon opened the Wonderland Theater at 253 King Street. It started out as a nickelodeon. They soon added a small auditorium in the rear of the building. Then, they enlarged the auditorium and eliminated the arcade machines. Others observed the popularity of this new form of entertainment. Soon King Street had the Dreamland, Fairyland, and Pictorum competing for an audience.

The Edisonia Theater opened in July, 1907 at 263 King Street. The owners offered a variety of entertainment. In addition to the various movie scenes, audiences were entertained by the Furst Band of the Artillery Corps and a series of illustrated songs.

All of these theaters had to compete with the vaudeville and legitimate theaters in town. George Brantley opened the Majestic Theater in June, 1908 at 343 King Street. This was primarily a vaudeville house, but often ran evenings of motion pictures. Films were beginning to tell stories. Audiences, who had grown tired of the unrelated reels of moving photographs, now expected films with a story, and recognizable actors, or movie stars.

But, too many theaters created a problem. No single theater was selling enough tickets to cover costs. In the summer of 1908, the theater owners met and agreed to form a corporation to manage the theater business in Charleston. Pastime Amusement Company was formed, with Albert Sottile as its President. The smaller theaters were closed and the others soon began to see profits increase.

As movie studios developed, a consistent source of new motion pictures evolved. Movie theaters were designed and built for the specific purpose of providing the best venue for showing these feature films. The Princess Theater at 304 King Street was the first establishment in Charleston to be built for the exclusive purpose of exhibiting motion pictures. Describing the new theater in 1913, Pastime Amusement Company stated to the newspaper, "In dedicating to the people of Charleston our latest advent in the pursuit of pleasure, we do so with the full conviction that it represents the near ideal we have long strived to obtain."

Princess Theater - photo about 1925

Garden Theater - 1918

Garden Theater - Interior 1918

That same year, Mr. Basil Kerr opened the Elco Theater at 549 King Street. John J. Miller opened the Dixie Land Theater at 616 King Street as a burlesque and movie theater for the African American community. The Colonial Theater opened the following year. While these theaters were better equipped and appointed, they were not grand.

On January 14, 1918, the Garden Theater opened at 371 King Street. At an opening ceremony, Albert Sottile said, "In the dedication of the Garden Theater, a hope long cherished is given visualization." The Garden Theater was indeed grand for its time. When one entered the Garden they walked across a tiled entrance under a huge ornate arch and into a garden of hanging flower baskets, caged singing canaries, trellises and crystal chandeliers.

The Lincoln Theater, an African American stage and movie house, opened in 1920. Veteran theater owner and national newspaper columnist Damon Ireland Thomas moved to Charleston in 1923 and took over operation of the Lincoln Theater. He retained his position for the next thirty years.

By the mid-1920s, motion pictures were a national passion. The Hollywood studio system was in power. But, no major studio was interested in building one of their magical movie palaces anywhere in South Carolina. Pastime Amusement Company built the closest thing to a movie palace that Charlestonians would ever see. The Gloria Theater opened at 331 King Street on August 19, 1927.

Gloria Theater - 1937

Through a long grand lobby one proceeded along beautifully decorated walls, past colorful murals and marble sculptures, into a 2,000 seat auditorium with a huge domed ceiling complete with dark blue sky and bright twinkling stars. It was still the silent film era.

Gloria Theater - now Sottile Theater

The 1930s brought sound, and new movie theaters to Charleston. Basil Kerr and his son, Francis Kerr, opened the Palace Theater at 566 King Street in 1931. The Riviera Theater, an Art Deco treasure, opened on the site of the Academy of Music on January 15, 1939. Less than two years later, the American Theater opened with 900 seats at 446 King Street. The last movie theater built by Pastime Amusement Company in downtown Charleston opened on Liberty Street in 1948. It was called the Arcade Theater, but Albert Sottile always referred to it as his "Little Gem."

Riviera Theater Interior - 1939

The last single-screen movie theater Pastime Amusement Company built was the Ashley Theater, just south of peninsular Charleston. It might be described as the first suburban theater built by the company that had dominated the movie exhibition business since 1908.

There are no single-screen movie theaters left in Charleston. The American Theater is still standing. It is used as an event venue. The Riviera Theater is now a conference and convention space. The once grand Garden Theater has been chopped up and converted into a trendy clothing store. The Ashley Theater is now a pizza restaurant. The facade of the Princess Theater remains. A restaurant

American Theater - 1997

occupies the interior space. All of the others have been demolished, except for the Gloria Theater. The Gloria, or at least the large auditorium, survives. It was renamed the Sottile Theater by the College of Charleston, its current owner.

Mrs. Margaret Dingate played piano at the Majestic Theater in 1918, and the theater organ on opening night at the Gloria Theater in 1927. She lived through the entire period of the single-screen movie theater. Well into her nineties, she told us, in an interview in 1992, "People had a lot of fun. Everybody was jolly. I miss it."

The American Theater was used in the 2004 feature film "The Notebook" directed by Nick Cassavetes.

American Theater Interior - 1942

George S. Brantley and Florence Brantley

George Brantley and his wife Florence opened the first movie theater in Charleston, the Theatorium, at 321 King Street, in 1907. He leased the space on the ground level of the old American Hotel. They bought 114 kitchen chairs, which George nailed together into rows of seats. They covered boards with cheesecloth and hung it for the screen. Florence suggested a phonograph with a large horn on top of the ticket booth to attract attention.

On May 26, 1907, an article appeared in *The Sunday News* entitled, "Fine Moving Pictures and Illustrated Song." The article read as follows:

"The Theatorium, the first moving picture theatre in Charleston, continues to attract large audiences daily and nightly, and the standard of excellence set by the manager some months ago has been maintained.

A recent innovation has been the employment of a professional singer and pianist, who give popular songs during the intermissions. The Theatorium secured a good hold upon the community and will no doubt retain it."

Theatorium!

We Have Engaged For Limited Time Only,

Mr A. E. Barr,

The Celebrated Baritone of the West. Don't Fail to Hear Him.

In June, 1907 Brantley placed an advertisement in the Charleston *News and Courier* which read; "Theatorium, 321 King Street. A select place of amusement for Ladies and children. Pictures and Illustrated Songs. – Changed Every Day – Admission 5 cents. White People Only."

Around September or October, 1907, ticket sales began to decline. George told Florence that he believed the movie theatre business was a fad that had played out. George sold the Theatorium to John C. Sherrill and A.T. Jennings for $5,000.

On November 29, 1907, George S. Brantley purchased the Theatorium in Wilmington, NC. The project failed and George S. Brantley returned to movie theater projects in Charleston, SC.

In February, 1908, he leased 343 King Street for a new theatre he would call the Majestic.

Later in 1908, he opened The New Theatorium on the east side of King Street just below Society Street. With so many theaters in operation, no one was making a profit. In the summer of 1908, George joined James and Albert Sottile, John C. Sherrill, and A.T. Jennings to form Pastime Amusement Company.

George became General Manager of all the theaters operated by Pastime Amusement Company. They closed two of the theaters and negotiated better prices from film distributors. The new venture began to show a profit.

In 1912, George sold his interest in Pastime Amusement Company to Albert Sottile. He opened White Swan Laundry at 1060 King Street. He never returned to the movie exhibition business.

He died in 1936 at the age of fifty-nine. Florence died in 1972.

Albert Sottile

Born in Sicily in 1880, Albert Sottile came to Charleston in 1891. "I came here because my older brother had already found Charleston and found it to be a good place for a young man to get along in the world."

The Pastime Amusement Company

In 1908, relations between the three groups showing movies in Charleston, according to Albert Sottile, "was bitter and unfriendly and it developed into a fight of extermination. Gradually, as they all became satisfied that they were playing a losing game, a spirit of trying to get together to solve their problem developed among them and at this juncture, I was invited to sit in with them, in the capacity of a mutual friend and ways and means of forming a merger were the subject of discussion."

The developments of the next few years cannot be told better than in the words of Albert Sottile. The following is compiled from letters, articles and notes written by him.

"In the summer of 1908. it was agreed that a stock company would be formed with a capital of $35,000 which would purchase the interests represented by the three groups. They would, in turn, be given Common Stock in payment so that; Brantley received 40% of the stock, his contribution being the Majestic and the New Theatorium; James Sottile received as his share 40% of the stock, his contribution being the Wonderland and The Idle Hour; Messrs. Sherrill and Jennings received 20% of the stock, their contribution represented by the old Theatorium. Thus, birth was given to Pastime Amusement Company and in compliance to the urgent demands made by all interested parties; I became its first president.

Albert Sottile

Immediate action was taken in curtailing expenses and of the five places, two of them converted into stores and with the elimination of competitive bidding and the closing of these two theaters (the New Theatorium and Idle Hour), the operation began at once to show a profit.

George Brantley was retained as General Manager, having direct charge of the Majestic operation and Mr. J.E. Sherrill was retained as manager of the Theatorium and of the Wonderland Theater. There were no other small theaters in operation at the time, though later, small places were opened and operated by local people.

In the fall of 1910, I bought 84-86 Society Street. In the spring of 1911, The Victoria Theater with two floors, an orchestra and balcony, came to life as the house of refined vaudeville."

With the opening of the Victoria Theater, Albert Sottile began his ascent as the "King of the motion picture theater business in Charleston." Albert Sottile served as president of Pastime Amusement Company until his death in 1960.

A.W. Petit

Mr. Arthur Washington Petit was born on September 15, 1862. He owned a dry goods store at 549 King Street and a toy store at 522 King Street.

In 1913, Mr. Petit opened the Elco Theatre in his former dry goods store at 549 King Street. He and his family lived above the theatre. He was one of the pioneers in bringing serial moving pictures to Charleston. Mr. Petit was well known and highly regarded by the citizens of Charleston. He died on January 15, 1934.

A.W. Petit

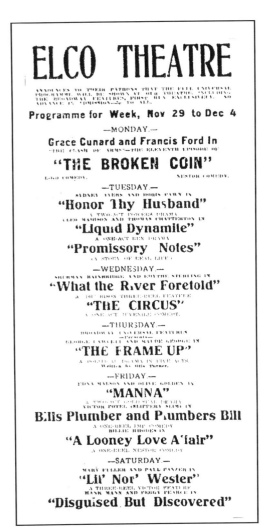

Newspaper Advertisement 1915

Handbill for the 1920 movie "Out of the Dust" courtesy of Mr. Brian Petit.

Damon Ireland Thomas

D. Ireland Thomas ran the Lincoln Theater in Charleston beginning in the early 1920's. He was born in 1875, near New Orleans. In 1900, he managed the Bijou Theater in Tampa, Florida. By 1904, he was managing a tent show for entertainment entrepreneur, Patrick H. Chappelle.

In 1916, Mr. Thomas was the New Orleans District manager for the Lincoln Motion Picture Company's national film distribution organization.

In 1919, Mr. Thomas and Mr. Harry Gant co-directed "A Man's Duty" for the Lincoln Motion Picture Company. For much of the early 1920's Mr. Thomas wrote a weekly column on motion pictures for the *Chicago Defender*, a leading national African American newspaper.

Mr. Thomas helped organize the Theater Owners Booking Association (T.O.B.A.), an African American vaudeville circuit. He was very committed to the community. He donated land for a new fire station and for a school.

Damon Ireland Thomas

Lincoln Theater
shortly before it was torn down

Lincoln Theater Exterior Concession Booth

Francis B. Kerr

Many Charlestonians remember him as the manager of the Palace Theatre at 566 King Street. During the 1940's and 1950's he carried on the movie traditions, started by his father Basil R. Kerr, who opened the Palace Theatre in 1931 as a combination vaudeville and movie theater. Francis Kerr once said, "During the Great Depression, people found it cheaper to spend hours in the theater than to go home and heat their homes. So, in actuality, we were their home-away-from-home."

As Hollywood was designing "Cinemascope" in 1955, Francis and his father came out with their own three-dimensional screen, which they patented. The Palace Theatre closed in 1957 and was torn down in 1968.

Photograph supplied by Francis B. Kerr, Jr.

CHESTER

We are endebted to Mrs. Malcolm L. Marion, Jr., of Chester, for much of this information. She conducted extensive research on buildings in Chester. She related to us the tragedy of the 1929 fire at the local library in which many issues of *The Chester Reporter* were destroyed.

In a diary, kept by Kate Gaston Davidson of Chester, Mrs. Marion found an entry of interest. On October 7, 1913, Mrs. Davidson wrote, "Bobby shed some tears over not going to the moving pictures last night. It's our rule not to go on school nights, but he's heard this was something extra." So, we can be fairly certain that movies were shown in Chester before 1913.

Advertisements for the Dreamland Theatre can be found in surviving issues of *The Chester Reporter* from 1915 through 1919. According to Mrs. Marion's research, Hill's Dreamland Theatre is listed at 103 Wylie Street in the City Directories 1920-1921 and 1924-1925. Roland G. Hill of Greensboro, NC, is listed as proprietor.

In the late 1920s or early 1930s, Mr. Joseph Walters ran the Dreamland Theatre. He changed the name to The City Theatre. Around 1935, Mr. Fred J. Powell moved to Chester. He bought The City Theatre. In 1939, Powell built a new movie theatre at 163 Main Street. He named this the Chester Theatre. It had an adjoining soda shop.

Mr. Powell renovated The City Theatre on Wylie Street and called it the Powell Theatre. For a short time, he also operated a small theatre at 127 Gadsden Street called the Palmetto Theatre. The Chester Theatre on Main Street was demolished around 1969.

Powell Theater - Photo taken in 2002

Advertisement for Dreamland Theatre
November, 2, 1915.

CHERAW

The Lyric Theater opened on Christmas day in 1920. Built by local pharmacist, Dr. James Ladd, this theater changed names over the years. It was known as the Cheraw Theatre, the Cheraw Cinema, and is now beautifully restored and is called the Theatre on the Green.

When it opened as a silent movie house, it had an open alcove into which a patron entered from the street. In the alcove was a ticket booth. After purchasing a ticket, which cost 11 cents in 1924, one entered the auditorium through double doors. Movies were sometimes accompanied by piano and other times by a record player.

There was no concession stand. Local patrons brought what they wanted to eat. They often purchased snacks from Mr. Ladd's drugstore.

In the summer of 1929, Cheraw audiences were treated to their first "talking picture," at the Lyric Theater. It was MGM's Oscar winning "The Broadway Melody." It was cool inside the theater due to the air conditioning system, which consisted of air blown by fans across large blocks of ice on the second floor.

By 1935, ticket prices had climbed to 15 cents. By the beginning of World War II, the admission for an adult reached twenty-five cents. And the theater was known as the Cheraw Theatre.

In the 1930s and 1940s attendees saw a feature, a newsreel, and a short subject. On Saturdays, the feature was followed by an episode from a serial.

To increase attendance on Wednesday nights, prices were lowered and drawings were held.

Lyric Theater - Cheraw

During World War II, Bob Rogers, who owned the Cheraw Theatre, came up with a very clever idea. Capitalizing on the large number of people in the area for military training, he opened a bowling alley in a building at the end of Market Street. Behind the bowling alley he installed showers, for which he charged twenty-five cents. On the floor above the bowling alley, he opened the Bowling Theater. The soldiers could bowl, shower and watch a movie. That lasted only a short time.

In the mid-1950s, the popularity of television and the drive-in signaled the end of the local movie theaters. From that time through the 1980s, the theater changed hands several times. At some point it was renamed the Cheraw Cinema. It closed in 1987.

The Cheraw Development Corporation bought the building in 1988. Plans were made to raise funding and create a center for the performing arts, a community meeting place, and lecture hall.

Many of the architectural and decorative features of the original building were restored. The plaster moldings and tin ceilings in the foyer and auditorium were saved.

Cheraw Theater (formerly Lyric Theater) - Cheraw

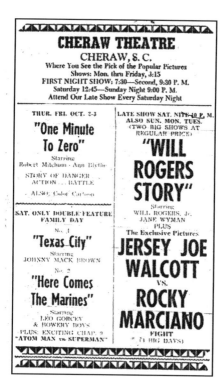

Cheraw Theater ad - 1951

The first staged event in the Theatre on the Green was performed by Cheraw's amateur dramatic group, On Stage. This opening brought life back into the old theater and mingled with the echoes of the audience that attended the opening of the old Lyric Theatre over seventy years earlier.

Our thanks to Sarah Spruill, Cheraw Visitors Bureau, for materials on the theater's history.

Statue near Theater on the Green of Dizzie Gillespie, who was born in Cheraw

Theater on the Green - Cheraw

CLINTON

We know of two movie theaters in Clinton. The Casino was located on South Broad Street next to the Masonic Temple. The Casino Theater closed in 1948. The building is still there.

Casino Theater Photo Courtesy Laurens County Library

The Broadway Theater opened at 209 North Broad Street in 1948.

In the 1963 Yearbook for Presbyterian College there is an advertisement that reads: Compliments of Broadway Theater which has served P.C. "uns" with the best in entertainment for more than 25 years.

From the book "Growing Up as a Lint Head" by Bill Gaskins:

"One thing Chris loved was money. He liked to use his money to go to the Saturday matinee at the Broadway Theater in downtown Clinton. I spent many of my Saturdays at the Broadway Theater and Chris always sat on the front row. The code of conduct was well established at the Broadway and was well enforced. Chris was safe and we were too."

Broadway Theater around 1957

CLIO

Built around 1910 by Jefferson D. Edens, Sr., Edens Opera House included stores, offices, and an auditorium. Theater companies entertained crowds drawn from Clio and surrounding towns. The auditorium was on the second floor.

Clio, like many other small towns in South Carolina, enjoyed live entertainment from New York's Vaudeville and legitimate theater stages. These shows arrived by trains traveling from New York to Miami.

Edens Opera House - Clio

Marlboro Theater

The Marlboro Theater was located on Main Street. It is now Barbara Hubbard's rose garden. One can still see the outline of the old theater's roof on the side of the hardware store operated by Mr. and Mrs. Hubbard. Barbara said the floor slope was dug into the ground. When the lot where the theater once stood was excavated, tons of dirt and top soil were added to make the area a garden.

Average Movie Ticket Prices

During our research we talked to many people who recalled that movie tickets cost 25 cents. Many factors explain this figure. Most of the people we interviewed had long memories. Ticket prices were lower in South Carolina than in more populated areas of the country. Average prices below include discounts and special pricing. Even when movies tickets cost 25 cents, some movies, like "Gone With The Wind" cost a dollar or more per ticket.

Year	Avg. Price
2011	$7.93
2008	$7.18
2003	$6.03
1999	$5.08
1988	$4.11
1983	$3.15
1975	$2.05
1970	$1.55
1969	$1.42
1966	$1.09
1965	$1.01
1962	$0.70
1956	$0.50
1954	$0.45
1945	$0.35
1935	$0.24
1924	$0.25
1910	$0.07

Source:
Motion Picture Association of America.

COLUMBIA

Almost all of Columbia's movie theaters were on Main Street. The Columbia Opera House, on the northwest corner of Main and Gervais Streets, was the first theater to regularly show movies. This was an occasional break from the usual live shows there.

By 1910, Columbia had two movie theaters on Main Street; the Lyric and the Grand. Soon, the Ideal Theater was attracting patrons in the 1300 block of Main. These theaters were soon joined by the Rialto.

In the 1920s the Ideal Theater offered a full orchestra accompanying the silent films. Theaters opened, closed, and changed names with some regularity. No one today would recall them, but they were the Pastime, Rivoli, Dreamland and Majestic. The most popular of the time was the Imperial Theater in the 1400 block of Main.

"The Jazz Singer" was shown in July, 1928 at the Ritz Theater. This was the first "talkie" shown in Columbia. The Ritz had recently been built on the space formerly occupied by the Ideal Theater. The Ritz was grand, with seating for 870 people.

By the beginning of the 1930s, movies were America's favorite entertainment. The Columbia Theater, formerly the Columbia Opera House, changed its name in 1931 to the Carolina Theater. While it now showed motion pictures primarily, it still offered live shows. The Rex Theater opened across the street from the Carolina.

In 1936 the State Theater opened in the 1600 block of Main Street and the Rex closed. The Rex was remodeled and reopened as the Strand Theater. But, the major theater to open on Main Street was

This is a poster from the collection of Malcolm Samuel Suggs, City Manager of the seven Columbia theatres in the Wilby-Kincey Theatre Chain. The hand painted poster is promoting "True to the Navy" to be exhibited at the Ritz Theater, June 9, 10, and 11, 1930.

the Palmetto Theater. It was built on the site of the former Imperial. It was the closest thing Columbia ever had to a real movie palace. It had seating for 1,600. It was air-conditioned. And, it was beautifully decorated.

Around 1939, the Carolina (formerly Opera House and Columbia Theater) was torn down to build the Wade Hampton Hotel.

As America geared up for World War II, the federal government encouraged cities near military bases to open the movie theaters on Sundays. On September 1, 1941 the new Carolina Theater opened a few doors north of the Wade Hampton Hotel. The 1940s may have been the high water mark for movie theaters and movie attendance in Columbia. There were five movie theaters operating on Main Street.

There was also the Five Points Theater on Harden Street which served a large and affluent community there. There were two African American theaters operating at the time; the Carver Theater on Harden Street near Benedict College and the Capitol Theater on Washington Street near Assembly.

The theaters and theater business remained fairly stable for the next twenty years. Segregation continued. Even though television arrived in Columbia in 1953, it didn't diminish the popularity of the movies. Cinemascope and stereophonic sound also arrived in Columbia in 1953 at the Palmetto Theater.

The Strand slowly fell into disrepair and disrepute. By the time it closed in 1958, it was showing burlesque films with strippers such as Tempest Storm and Lili St. Cyr. The State Theater closed in 1961, but became the Fox Theater. The site of the Strand also became a new movie house in 1968, called the Miracle Theater.

What really killed the downtown movie theaters in Columbia was "the burbs." The suburban Atlantic Twin and the Richland Mall theaters opened in the 1960s. Even so, another new movie theater opened on Main Street in 1970. The first movie at the new Jefferson Square Theater was "Tora, Tora, Tora." At that time, Columbia had six active movie theaters on Main Street.

Then, one-by-one, they began to close. The Miracle and Palmetto closed down in 1979. The Ritz, which had become the Plaza III during the 1970s, closed in 1980. The Carolina survived until 1983, mostly by featuring Kung-Fu movies. The Fox, which had been converted into two screens, one in the auditorium and one in the balcony, closed in 1987.

On Sunday, May 15, 1993, the last picture show on Main Street, the Jefferson Square Theater closed.

Fox Theater in the 1970s. This will be the home of the Nickelodeon and a favorite spot for movies. Main Street will have one of its theaters back in business.

The Palmetto Theater - 1939

Photo courtesy of David Suggs from the collection of Malcolm Samuel Suggs,
City Manager of the seven Columbia theatres in the Wilby-Kincey Theatre Chain.

For more photographs of Columbia Theaters from this collection,
including the Carolina Theater, Ritz Theater, Strand Theater
and 5 Points Theater, go to pages 132 - 134.

Malcolm Samuel Suggs

Before moving to South Carolina in 1937, Sam Suggs managed movie theaters in Alabama, Tennessee, and Virginia. He was City Manager of the seven Columbia Theatres (Palmetto, Ritz, Strand, Carolina, 5 Points, Star-Lite Drive-In and later the Richland Mall) in the Wilby-Kincey Theatre Chain, which was based in Charlotte, NC. He became Distric Manager of the Palmetto Theater Company after the retirement of Warren Irvin in the late 1960s. Mr. Irvin described Mr. Suggs as "one of the finest theater men in the South."

Describing the qualities of a good theater manager, Suggs said, "He's got to have the ability to feel the pulse of the theater-going public and know what it likes. In other words, he's got to keep forever young. If he doesn't, he will get behind the times."

During a Savings Bond Rally in Columbia in 1942, a huge crowd gathered to see the Hollywood star, Betty Grable. Mr.Suggs was to accompany Ms. Grable from the rally on Main Street to an appearance for the troops at Fort Jackson. When Ms. Grable got into the back seat with Mr. Suggs, the crowd swarmed around the car making it impossible to move. It took an hour for the police to get the crowd under control. Mr. Suggs always smiled when he recalled that story. "I was trapped in the back seat of a car for an hour with Betty Grable!"

Sam Suggs retired in 1974, after spending 47 years in the film industry. He saw motion pictures evolve from the silent era, through the "talkies" and from black and white to wide-screen technicolor.

Malcolm Samuel Suggs

Betty Grable in Columbia - 1942

CONWAY

We owe much of our knowledge of the movie theaters of Conway to William T. Goldfinch, whose wonderful first-person narrative, "Heyday of the Movies in Conway" appears in a 1995 issue of the Horry County Historical Society's publication, "The Independent Republic Quarterly."

Casino Theatre

The first movie theatre in Conway was the Casino Theatre located on Main Street north of Fourth Avenue. The original owner and theatre name are not known. It was purchased by Mr. McQueen Quattlebaum who named it the Casino. The earliest reference we have found is in the *Horry County Herald* dated April 1, 1915. A very large illustrated advertisement promoted the first episode of "The Million Dollar Mystery" a twenty-three episode serial. Admission was 5 cents and 10 cents.

According to Mr. Goldfinch, Mr. Quattlebaum closed the Casino Theatre when the Pastime opened.

Pastime Theatre

Located at 409 Main Street, he Pastime Theatre opened in November, 1916, showing "Gloria's Romance."

The Pastime Theatre was described by Mr. Goldfinch. "The front of the building was rather stark, lacking a marquee. Instead, it had a sign in the shape of a 'T' which hung out over the sidewalk. It said 'THEATRE' in large letters across the top and 'PASTIME' vertically beneath."

When the Pastime opened it was said to be a modern playhouse, the equal to any in a town of Conway's size. It was where the first sound movie played in Conway. The Pastime Theater closed in 1936 and was torn down in 1947.

Casino Theatre Ad
June 17, 1915

Carolina Theatre

The Carolina Theater opened at 408 Main Street on August 6, 1936. The lobby was large and attractive with a terrazzo floor, stamped metal ceiling, textured walls and the latest period lighting. Entrance to the lobby was off of Fourth Avenue.

The Carolina closed briefly in 1952 for renovation and reopened in 1953. Except for a fire that caused its closure for six weeks in 1964, the Carolina Theatre remained in operation until June 15, 1965.

NEW CAROLINA THEATRE OPENS

DEMOCRATS HOLD MEETING

Allow East and West Conway and Loris Later Time for Closing Polls

THE ROLLS ARE PURGED

Several New Precincts Get Voting Places Designated By the Committee

NEW BUILDINGS ADD BEAUTY TO CONWAY

The above picture shows the main entrance to the new Carolina Theatre. On the left are two storerooms recently remodeled by Mr. H. G. Cushman. On the right of the theatre are two storerooms owned by Bagnor Bros.

Beautiful New Theatre, One of Finest In the State, Opens Today, Thursday

SOUND SYSTEM THE VERY BEST

GROWERS LOOK FOR INCREASE

CRASH OF CARS KILLS SEVERAL

LONG LIST OF CANDIDATES

Headline news when Carolina Theater opened in Conway - August 6, 1936

Holliday Theatre

Opened October 1, 1947, the Holliday Theater was located at 335 Main Street. The theatre was built by Joseph W. Holliday and John Monroe J. Holliday as a memorial to their father. It had 650 seats, a "cry" room for mothers with small children, and certain seats were said to be larger than others to accommodate more robust patrons.

The Holliday Theatre abruptly closed in 1948 and reopened in 1952. It closed again in 1953 and reopened in 1954. Then, in 1955, it closed for ten years. It reopened for eleven months as a second-run theatre.

In 1965, the theatre was completely renovated. By the time it closed, in 1986, it had deteriorated. In January, 1990, it was destroyed by fire.

It has since been rebuilt as the Main Street Theatre, home of the reportory group, Theatre of the Republic.

Holliday Theater
1950s

COTTAGEVILLE

Boiled Peanuts and a Movie

The Cottageville Theater was opened on May 28, 1941 by Mr. Harry Reeves (1904-1966). Mr. Reeves' daughter, Mrs. James Cockfield, told us about the theater when we visited her in 2007.

She recalled that the theater used a 16mm projector which her father purchased from a shop on Broad Street in Charleston. She operated the projector occasionally. Other times she sold tickets and boiled peanuts to the customers. They never had popcorn at the theater.

She remembered that the theater was open on Friday and Saturday nights. Sometimes it was open on Wednesday night. She said her father sometimes took the projector to the black school so the children there could see the movies.

The theater closed in the early 1960s. After the theater closed, it was a skating rink for a time. Then, for awhile, it was a Dime Store, and later, a thrift shop. More recently, it was a storage space.

Cottageville Theater

Southern Concessions

In addition to popcorn and candy bars, theaters in South Carolina sometimes offered boiled peanuts and "Chilly Dillys" promoted as "The Personality Pickle."

DARLINGTON

An article written by Mr. Shaler T. Stanley in 1996, gives a rich account of Darlington's movie theater history from 1909 until 1949. Mr. Stanley relates that the first movie theater in Darlington was the Bijou. It was opened in 1909, by James E. King and J.F. Byrd. Around 1910, Mr. Percy Fisher, of Florence, bought the Bijou, added mirrors in the lobby and renamed it the Mirror Theater.

Around 1912, Mitchell and Richards, of Bennettsville, opened a movie theater they named The Blue Mouse. This movie theater had a big electric sign that flashed on and off saying, "Mutual Pictures Make Time Fly." A year or so later, it was renamed the Alamo Theater. In 1919, the Alamo Theater changed hands and was renamed the Dreamland Theater.

Before 1918, Earl Baxter, publisher of the *News and Press*, leased the Opera House in the Town Hall and opened it as the Liberty Theater. George Hendrickson bought the Liberty Theater from Baxter in 1919. In 1921, Earl Baxter and Bert Prescott opened a theater on Pearl Street called The Rex. That same year, a theater chain in North Carolina acquired the lease on the Liberty Theater and changed the name to the Carolina Theater. This operation lasted only a short time and George Hendrickson was offered the lease and resumed operation of the Liberty Theater.

In 1929, a Western Electric sound system was added to the Liberty Theater. At first, business was brisk. But, as the Great Depression lingered, Hendrickson came close to closing the theater several times.

Wilby-Kincey Theatres bought half interest in the Liberty Theater in 1936, and made major renovations. They advertised "Practically

Everything New - Including the phone number." Business improved steadily. By the time the United States entered World War II, crowds at the Liberty Theater stood an hour to get a ticket. Once in the lobby, they stood another hour to get a seat.

In 1948, Sam Irvin bought George Hendrickson's share of the Liberty Theater. He immediately began construction of a new theater on Pearl Street. This was called the Darlington Theater.

The Liberty Theater was torn down in January, 1965. The building that once housed the Darlington Theater is now an office space.

In August, 2008, while walking around Darlington's town square, we met Mr. Allen Thames in front of the drug store and asked him if he recalled the theaters. He pointed to the opposite side of the square and said the Liberty Theater used to be there. He remembered going there before World War II to play bingo and stay for the midnight show.

Site of Darlington Theater
on Pearl Street

Advertisement for the Liberty Theater promoting the major improvements done in 1936.
Courtesy of the Darlington County Historical Society.

DENMARK

Debra Heath Remembers
the Dane Theatre in Denmark

My fond childhood memory of a single screen theater is of the Dane Theatre in Denmark, SC. I have so very many memories of going to movies as a child at this theater. It was always so cool and dark and it had red velvet seats which I thought were beautiful. The ladies restroom had a vanity that I thought was so glamorous. "My seat" was always on the left side of the theater about half way down the aisle in the middle section.

Although The Dane Theatre was 10 miles away from where my family lived we attended very often. My Dad would never miss a John Wayne movie - we saw each and every one of them in The Dane Theatre.

One special memory is when I was eight years old and a group of my friends and I boarded the train one Saturday afternoon in Olar, SC, and rode the ten miles to Denmark to see the matinee which was "Old Yeller." I will never forget that thrill or the feeling because it was the first time I had ever ridden a train!

Mr. Lundy operated The Dane and he always sat in the tiny little window to take our money. I just can't ever remember seeing anyone else in that window but Mr. Lundy. I can remember paying a quarter to see many movies but I can't recall paying other amounts as the price changed as time went on.

I had a friend who loved scary movies like I did. When we went to see movies like "The Mummy" and "Dracula" in the Dane, I would hide my eyes at the really scary parts and she would tell me when it was safe to open my eyes - sometimes she would fool me and tell me to open them when something scary was still going on.

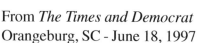

From *The Times and Democrat*
Orangeburg, SC - June 18, 1997

The Dane Theatre, built in 1947 and closed in 1979, has been completely restored to art deco splendor by the City of Denmark. The 454-seat theater is being utilized as a cultural center by the city, which is also leasing the facility to various organizations and groups for special events.

Dane Theatre restoration earns preservation award for Denmark

By CAROL B. BARKER
Times and Democrat Staff Writer

DENMARK, S.C. -The City of Denmark and the Denmark Downtown Development Association will receive a 1997 Preservation Honor Award at Brookgreen Gardens on June 29 for the restoration of the Dane Theatre in downtown Denmark.

The Palmetto Trust for Historic Preservation each year presents Preservation Honor Awards to a select group of South Carolinians who have made significant contributions to preserving the state's history.

Built in 1947, the Dane Theatre, which was owned by the Frank Lundy family, changed with the times by moving from showing classic westerns in the 1940s and 1950s starring people like John Wayne and Tex Ritter to movies like Steven Spielberg's modern classic "ET" in the 1970s.

The Dane Theatre closed for the last time in 1979 but remained a nostalgic land-mark for local residents who grew up going to Saturday matinees at the Dane.

With the vision of restoring the Dane Theatre for use as a cultural center, the Denmark Downtown Development Association launched a fund-raising campaign to purchase the property in the early 1990s. Spear-headed by Paula Brooker Guess, the effort succeeded in raising the $20,000 needed to buy the Dane from the Lundy family.

The DDDA then gave the property to the City of Denmark, which undertook its restoration.

Bill Fudge, DDDA manager, said the City of Denmark spent approximately $36,000 to restore the Dane to its original art deco splendor.

"That doesn't include $42,000 for a new air-conditioning and heating system, which is being paid for by the City of Denmark through a long-term financing arrangement with SCE&G," Fudge said.

To help finance the project, he said many people "bought seats" in the theater for $50 each. Names of those purchasing seats were placed on engraved plaques that were attached to the backs of the seats.

Originally, the Dane had a total of 720 seats, including those on the ground level and in the balcony. The restoration and addition of a performance stage left a capacity of 454 seats.

"The city was able to keep the cost of the restoration project way down, because city employees Archie Williams and Bob Graham did much of the interior work such as enlarging the stage, all the interior painting and refurbishing the seats," Fudge pointed out.

Now that its restoration is complete, he said the city is having no trouble leasing the Dane Theatre to various organizations and groups.

"It's become a very popular place to hold special events and is being rented almost every weekend," Fudge said. "The acoustics in the Dane are terrific, which makes it an ideal place to hold concerts, gospel programs and other musical events."

Fudge said the DDDA has received calls from all over the state since word has spread of Denmark's Preservation Honor Award for the Dane Theatre restoration.

"We're getting calls from all over the state from people wanting advice on restoring old theaters," he said.

This is not the first honor the Dane's restoration has won for the City of Denmark this year.

In March, Denmark was presented the 1997 Citation for Community Commitment by the S.C. Downtown Development Association.

"Everybody who has worked on the restoration of the Dane is so proud," Fudge said.

DILLON

The 1913 *Cahn Hill Directory of Theaters* states that Dillon had a population of 2,000. The only theater mentioned is the "It" Theater. This theater was on the ground floor and had a balcony. The proscenium was twenty-two feet wide and the stage was thirty feet wide. It Theater had two dressing rooms for live traveling shows. It likely exhibited movies when they were available.

The 1921 *Cahn Hill Directory* does not list the "It" Theater but does list Everybodys Theater as a motion picture theater. The Sanborn Map of 1924 shows it located at 114 North Railroad Avenue. The 1927 edition of *Film Yearbook* lists only the Everybodys Theater with a seating capacity of 300.

Ritz Theater Opens June 30, 1930
Florence Morning News

Dillon, S.C. June 25
Dillon's latest enterprise is the new Ritz Theatre equipped with the Delores Phonofilm Sound System. The Temple Theater, Inc. B.R. Berry of Hartsville, General Manager, is the owner of the new Dillon amusement plant with B.B. Benefield of Dillon, veteran picture show manager as resident manager. This phonofilm sound system has no superior in variety of high class entertainment.

The September 27, 1934 edition of *The Field,* of Conway, published the following article:

New Theater for Dillon in Future

Dillon, Sept. 22 – The building on Railroad Avenue, formerly occupied by the Every Bodys Theater has been torn away to make room for another modern theater for motion pictures in Dillon, to be owned and operated by the Anderson Theater Company. This building is one of a group of business houses recently purchased by H.H. Anderson of Dillon and Cheraw from the Jefferson Standard Life Insurance Company as a spot cash transaction running into money in excess of twenty one thousand dollars.

B.B. Benfield's Broadway Theater on West Main Street is another modern motion picture show house just completed a little more than a year ago and is still doing a very profitable business.

The Dillon Theater had a seating capacity of 450 while the Broadway Theater, at 106 West Main Street, seated 300.

The 1945 edition of *Film Daily Yearbook* lists both the Dillon Theater and Broadway Theater.

Apparently Everybodys Theater was built around 1919, at 110 North Railroad Avenue (now MacArthur Avenue) as a movie theater. It was torn down in 1934 and a new theater was built on the site. This was the Dillon Theater, a building of Spanish Colonial design that is now the Dillon County Theater.

Dillon County Theater
Photo courtesy of Jim Verrier

EASLEY

The story of the movie theaters of Easley is the story of the Armistead family. The following section, on the Armistead family, is both unique and typical of movie theater owners in South Carolina. You will understand how both statements can be true when you read it. It was provided to us by John A. Armistead of Gafney, grandson of Egbert A. Armistead, Sr., and son of Harold E. Armistead, Jr. We have included the story as he wrote it without editing. It is a first-hand account that captures the specific details and broader influences of the movie theater business in our state. We are very grateful to him for sharing his observations.

Movies and the Armistead Family
by John A. Armistead

Though I'm not a historian, per se, I have a good memory for the institution of "main street" movie theatres during the prosperous 1950s and into the less prosperous mid to late 1960s. The latter decline, in large measure, can be attributed to the shift of populations away from city centers, and to the construction of newer theatres associated with shopping malls. The same demographic shifts affected not just movie theatres, but most businesses in town centers.

Before every home had one or more automobiles, a diversity of businesses could flourish in town centers, because people often could walk there to shop. When the automobile allowed traveling more afar to buy goods and services, the logic of having a diverse town center wasn't there any more. The parking meters that had provided income to towns and cities, suddenly became the final nail in the coffin to flourishing town centers. The "free parking" in malls was guaranteeing their economic success.

I had incidental contact with movie exhibitors from across the Carolinas when I accompanied my father, Harold E. Armistead, on a good number of his trips to Charlotte - both to book new movies, and to attend meetings of the Board of Directors of the Theatre Owners of North and South Carolina. On one such trip, I was introduced to Charleston's Albert Sottile, who bore a striking resemblance to my grandfather, Egbert Anderson Armistead, Sr. I recall how gracious he seemed. His friendship with my father directly affected me, because Mr. Sottile sent Daddy a huge box of chocolate candy every Christmas during the late 1940s to the mid 1950s.

Latta Arcade, a "pedestrian only" street, was on the north side of Tryon Street (Charlotte's "Main" street) and three blocks west of *the Square.* The flavor of those stores and shops was very European. About one forth of the businesses located there were allied to movie theatres in some way. On the second floor, facing Tryon Street, was the offices of the TOA. There were numbers of small conference rooms where movies could be booked, as well as a small theatre that could seat about forty people. I occasionally watched coming-attractions "trailers," and in some cases watched an entire 20-minute reel of a new movie being promoted. I even had lunch with one or more movie exhibitors that Daddy knew from across the Carolinas. Daddy was a past President of the NC & SC TOA. When I moved to Charlotte in 1971, several of the managers of theatres I patronized recalled Daddy, well.

Because my father knew so many people in the movie exhibiting business, on family trips we would sometimes stop in a town and Daddy would drop in to say hello to a friend who was the manager or owner of a particular movie theatre. It was a constant source of my pride that Daddy was so well-known and liked. He once got a letter delivered from out of state with just this address: Mr. Harold E. Armistead; South Carolina!

Harold E. Armistead, Jr.

I can infer from my father's personable nature that he learned to be that way from his father, Egbert. My father was just fourteen years old when his father died. But not before he had taught Daddy how to be gracious in dealing with movie patrons and with employees. While still in high school Daddy was managing Easley's Lyric Theatre. His mother, Nena Pearl Dacus Armistead, handled the cash. Those two were easily the most recognized people in Pickens County, for spending so much time in the ticket booth facing Main Street.

Before there were malls as places to hang-out, movie theatres were where parent's dropped-off their kids for the first show in the afternoon with enough popcorn and candy money to keep them going for four or more hours. With movies playing continually, there was little way of knowing when a person came in, other than for the usher (such as I was, part time, for nearly 17 years) to remember. That was important, because if someone became too restless or too loud, we would inform them that they had seen the movie already. But we always tried to be nice about maintaining order. I characterize movie ushers and managers during the pre-mall era as "baby sitters."

What we did was an important part of the social etiquette of thousands of kids who passed through our doors. Daddy even got a letter from one had-been trouble-maker, who after, getting religion, thanked Daddy for steering him more toward the straight and the narrow.

In many, many ways, the Lyric Theatre positively influenced our entire town and county. It had been "traditional" for town businesses to take a day off on Saturday, or to take at least half a day off on Saturday. Can you imagine how devastating it would be to a town center movie theatre if the town got deserted by 12:00 noon on Saturday, the one day when kids should be able to attend? My father saw that as a detriment with a solution. While still in grammar school, Daddy got recognized for being artistic. He had painted flowers and a mountain scene on large terra cotta pots that were on his family's front porch. Immediately, people seeing the artistic pots requested that Daddy paint similar pots for their front porches. One of the merchants in town asked Daddy if he could "letter" on his glass storefront? The answer was, "Of course!" Soon, Daddy was painting product information and prices for every store in town, and those often changed weekly. Daddy had a printed letterhead which reads: "I made 'signs' before I could talk!"

It was no problem for this gregarious and well-liked young man, Harold E. Armistead, to organize the Easley Business League, which would later become the Easley Chamber of Commerce. The spark for that organization was getting area merchants to agree to remain open until at least 5:00 p.m. on Saturday, in exchange for having all businesses close Wednesday afternoon. The positive effect on those businesses was immediate. Easley was a flourishing place on Saturdays! People drove here from afar just to walk among the crowds on our sidewalks!

During the Great Depression, people were cheered by going to movies. So, movie exhibitors were spared being out of work. My father's older brother, Colley Armistead, was out of work from his job working as a dispatcher for the railroad. To help his brother, and to expand the Armistead movie business, Daddy designed an approximate 150 seat Lyric movie theatre for the town of Honea Path, SC. Banks were failing right and left, but the 'safe' construction loan on the new theatre, apparently, was instrumental in helping the Honea Path Bank survive. Colley's son, Frank, told of being invited to a shareholders meeting of that bank, and being treated royally. Successes can beget successes! Movie theatres are no small part of the economy.

In the early days, Hollywood was turning out enough new movies to run three movies per week. But there were lower per-day costs for movie rental if each movie was run for four days. So, Daddy booked movies for both Lyric theatres. Those ran in Easley the first two days and in Honea Path the second two days. Carolina Delivery Service, Inc., in Charlotte, was a CRUCIAL and most reliable part of the success of motion picture exhibiting in the Carolinas!

The show couldn't go on unless there were reels of film being picked-up and delivered with perfection. CDS did just that! But the cost for delivering film from Easley to Honea Path was high. To save money, my Uncle Colley Armistead made six over-an-hour-long trips to and from Easley per week. When the economy improved enough so that the railroad business needed him, he turned theatre management over to his sister, Dora Armistead Higgins, who, on Valentine's Day 1947, married a former Seabee from the 'Pacific Theatre.' He was her employee, Pete Dugan.

Pete Dugan, photographer, became well-known. He got started in that business because my father, who was a part-time professional photographer before WWII, had the needed equipment unused in the large upstairs office of the Easley Lyric Theatre. Daddy had to decide between being a photographer and being a theatre owner. He chose the latter.

His father, Egbert, had moved his family from town to town in Georgia and Florida to capitalize on the new appeal of, first, reels of film viewed by one person at a time, and later, projected movies on screens. Egbert opened one of the first conventional, non-converted stage theatres in the USA. Such was in Social Circle, Georgia. He modified an existing level-floor brick building that is still there as of this writing. The wooden floor was jacked up off of its piers to cause the desired slope to the floor. A similar jacking "down" (rather than up) was done at the Lyric in Easley.

None of the five or six theatres Egbert had run was built new. That was a goal in his life which was latter fulfilled by the construction of the Colony Theater on West Main Street in Easley. The building contract exceeded $150,000.00 in 1947.

The design included a small restaurant on the second floor and a coffee shop on the first floor. Though the quality of both was excellent, public bias toward established businesses necessitated their being closed. Fortunately, the space was soon converted to the offices of an accountant.

Harold E. Armistead was a champion of the cause of fairness in motion picture exhibiting. He didn't think it was fair to allow cities like Greenville to book pictures before those same films could be available in Easley. By the mid 1960s Hollywood was turning out less than 1/3 the number of films that it did in the 1940s. That allowed movie exhibitors less choices of which movies they could show. Some of the distributing companies resorted to essential blackmail: Book "my" picture at "my" price, or you will have no movie to show… at all.

In the early years, movie salesmen were gentlemen. They actually made appointments and would come to each individual theatre. Later, once highways improved, movie managers had to do the traveling, like to Charlotte.

Movies with the likes of Elvis Presley, John Wayne, Doris Day, Rock Hudson, Jimmy Stewart, Marilyn Monroe, Debbie Reynolds, etc. etc. kept main street theatres alive for a while. However, most of the joy of movie exhibiting had drained away at least 25 years before the Colony Theater closed its doors. Perhaps, when town centers are re-invented by rare visionaries, the glamour of sharing movie-viewing experiences with one's friends, neighbors and acquaintances will return.

Surely, nothing can match live audience reactions to the dramas or the terrors that are being depicted on the screen. And nothing can match seeing the tears in the eyes of fellow movie goers leaving the theatres, be that from joy or from sadness.

Colony Theater in Easley

John A. Armestead and his mother in front of the Lyric Theater in Easley in 1951

EDGEFIELD

The Edgefield Theatre is listed in the 1921 edition of *The Julius Cahn – Gus Hill Theatrical Guide and Moving Picture Directory*. The directory states that the population of Edgefield in 1921 was 1,771.

The Augusta Chronicle
December 8, 1935

In an article about the Trenton P.T.A., it is noted that, "Through the courtesy of Mr. Chas. Hammond, manager of the Edgefield Theatre, every member of the tenth grade will be presented a ticket to a picture show for having the greatest number of parents at the meeting. Mr. Hammond will continue the offer throughout the school year."

The Augusta Chronicle
January 10, 1936

Edgefield Theatre Will Change Hands
The Edgefield moving picture theatre will pass under a new ownership Monday, January 13. Sam Hammond who has been operating The Strand Theatre for the past year and a half has sold his interest to Alber Berelowitz of Whitmire, who now operates two theatres, one at Whitmire and one at Lockhart.

The theatre will be closed the early part of next week for improvements, the first picture under the management is planned for Thursday, January 16. Mr. Berelowitz will make frequent visits to Edgefield and will have a resident manager, Frank Bryan of Charlotte.

The Film Daily Yearbook – 1945, lists Edgefield as having the Towne Theatre with a seating of 200.

ELLENTON

The first movie theater in Ellenton was a tent show. The hand-cranked projector provided movies to a crowd of fifty to one hundred patrons. The theater was run by Mr. White. In 1938, Mr. Mills, his wife, and their son, Lee Murray, drove from Varnville, SC, twice a week to provide movies to the people of Ellenton. The theater they constructed had no roof. The sides were made of a wooden frame covered with burlap bags so no one on the outside could watch the movies. Eventually, a strong rain storm caused the flimsy building to collapse.

Mr. Sid O'Berry built a theater a few years later in an old store building on Main Street. The interior had seating on one side for whites and the other side for African Americans. There was a dividing rail down the center of the theater to provide segregation.

O'Berry's Ellenton Theater

By 1953, the entire town of Ellenton had disappeared. Everyone had to move away. It is the only city in the United States to be taken by the government to build a nuclear site. Today, it is the Savannah River Site.

ELLOREE

Dr. Robert E. Holman of Elloree, author of "The Black Bag," World War II Veteran, and town doctor, shared memories of Elloree's movie theaters.

The first movie theater in Elloree was the Blue Bird Theatre on Cleveland Street, owned by a Mr. Heatley. Films were of the silent variety. An automatic player piano furnished the proper music.

A well meaning lady was the self-appointed reader of titles and quotations flashed on the screen. Those who could read sat as far away from her as possible. Those who could not sat closer to her.

When this theater closed, movies were shown in a tent by traveling operators. These movies were mostly two reelers and westerns with a few cops and robbers. Patrons usually sat on benches. The first reel was shown, followed by numerous commercials for local merchant sponsors and then the final reel was shown.

The Playland Theatre was opened in 1937. It was owned by Dr. J.T. Green. The first location was in the building occupied now by Hall's Dime Store.

Mrs. J.T. Green sold tickets. Javan Shedd ran the projector. Others employed in some capacity were Keitt Brandenburg, J.R. Bardin, Robert Jones, Bob Hill and Robert Dantzier.

In 1941 the theatre was built across the street and the movies moved. The coming of television spelled doom for the small town theatres across the country, and the Playland Theatre was one of the victims.

ESTILL

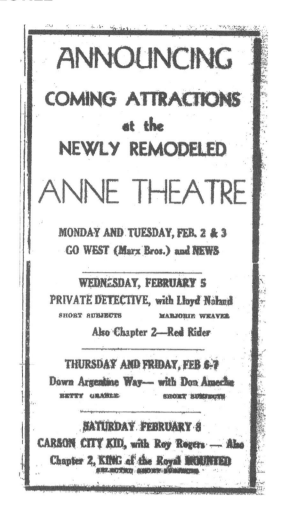

Estill had the Anne Theater. This advertisement from 1941 shows that there was a movie on Monday and Tuesday with a newsreel; a movie on Wednesday with short subjects and a chapter of a serial; a movie on Thursday and Friday with a short subject, and a Western with Roy Rogers on Saturday with a short subject and an episode of a serial. No movie was shown on Sunday.

By 1955, the Anne had been renamed the Estill Theater and matinees were being offered on Sundays. The newsreels, short subjects and serials had been dropped from the schedule.

FAIRFAX

The Augusta Chronicle - March 16, 1936

Talent Contest Won
By Miss McSweeney

Miss Marjorie McSweeney, 12-year-old daughter of Mr. and Mrs. Ray Stuckey, and granddaughter of Dr. and Mrs. F.H. Boyd, of Allendale, received a cash award as first prize over 28 other contestants in an amateur talent contest at the Pal Theatre in Fairfax this week. Her name will be submitted to a New York theatrical agency which conducts a "Search for Talent" every year. Her number, a song and tap-dance, brought down the house with applause.

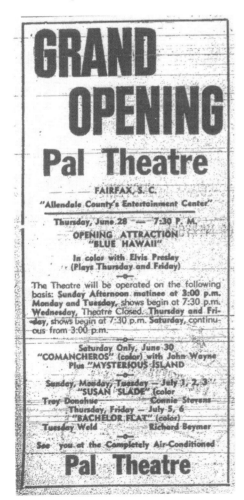

Pal Theater ad - June, 1962

Sneaking into the Movies

for Free

Cathy Kennedy recalled collecting nickels and pennies from her girl friends until they had enough to buy one ticket to the movie theater on Sullivan's Island. The girl who bought a ticket would go into the women's restroom and open the window so the other girls could climb in. One by one, they would come out and find a seat in the dark.

One woman recalled sneaking into the Gloria Theater in Charleston. She tied a string to the curtain on the left side of the screen. She ran the string to the right side of the screen where the "Exit" door was located. Then, she tugged on the string and made the curtain move. When the usher came to investigate, she opened the "Exit" door. While the usher looked behind the curtain, her friends snuck in for free.

FLORENCE

O'Dowd's Theater opened in the City Hall auditorium in 1911. In 1919, it moved to 115 South Dargan Street. At that time, Mr. M.F. Schnibbens opened the Colonial Theater in City Hall. O'Dowd's Theater closed in December, 1933, when Mr. J.M. O'Dowd retired from the movie business. The Carolina Theater opened in the same location on December 24, 1933. It was opened by Mr. M.F. Schnibbens. The following article appeared in the *Morning News* on December 23, 1933.

O'Dowd Praises New Carolina On Eve of Opening

A name long familiar in electric lights on the business streets of Florence has bowed to the magic wand of changing time and in place of O'Dowd's on Christmas Day will flash "Carolina," Florence's new and modern picture palace.

While we welcome the new we cannot help but remember the long years of enjoyment given us by Mr. J.M. O'Dowd, one of the pioneers in the motion picture industry in this state.

Mr. O'Dowd began his entertainment career in Orangeburg in 1906 moving to Florence in 1911, where for several years he conducted the O'Dowd's Theater in the City Hall auditorium now occupied by the Colonial Theatre. In 1915 he built, on South Dargan Street, one of the most attractive show places in the state. This theater has been undergoing a complete renovation of the past thirty days and will reopen on Christmas day under the name of Carolina and under the management of M.F. Schnibbens.

Mr. O'Dowd in retiring from his life-long vocation stated that he was prompted in leasing his theater by the ever increasing demands made upon his time as manager of the *Morning News*. He will now devote his entire time in endeavoring to give the residents of the Pee Dee area a bigger and better newspaper.

Mr. O'Dowd also stated the new management of the new Carolina has exceeded their promises in improving his property and that the new effects are amazingly attractive. He also stated that Mr. Schnibbens could not have found a more fitting picture to open the new theater with than "Little Women." It's Mr. O'Dowd's opinion that there never has been a more entertaining and wholesome picture made than the one in which Katherine Hepburn's star reaches its sublimest heights.

M. F. Schnibbens' Comments

It is not very often that an entire city can receive a mutual Christmas present. But in the opening of the Carolina theatre the city of Florence will receive a gift that every true Florentine will be more than proud of.

I will not go into detail to describe the improvements that have been made on the theatre for that would spoil your surprise, but I will say that, with the opening of the Carolina, Florence will have a theatre as beautiful as any in the Carolinas.

Along with "Little Women" the Carolina Theater showed Disney's *Silly Symphony*, "The Three Little Pigs" as a cartoon short. At this time, Mr. Schnibbens began operating both the Carolina Theater and the Colonial Theater.

Mr. Schnibben arrived in Florence in 1915. He made many improvements to the City Auditorium since leasing the property in 1919 and ran the Colonial Theater at that location since that time.

The Roxy Theater opened on November 23, 1939. It ran both live shows and motion pictures. The 1945 edition of *Film Daily Yearbook* lists the Carolina and the Colonial, each with 750 seats. Additionally, the directory lists the Lincoln, Roxy and State, each with 300 seats.

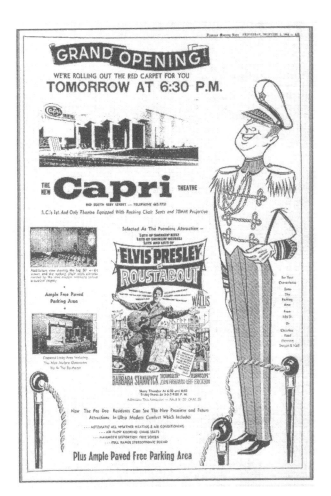

Capri Opens - December 2, 1961

Rocking chair seats, a specially designed carpet, and the state's first 70 millimeter projection equipment are three features combining to give Pee Dee movie fans the most modern conveniences when the Capri Theatre swings open its doors Thursday.

The Capri, with an auditorium measuring 66 x 105 feet, contains an even 700 seats. The theater is also equipped to carry six track, transistorized stereophonic sound through five speakers behind the screen and 10 surrounding speakers on the walls. You will enjoy the auditorium with its tasteful décor and, one more symbol that vaudeville is dead; there is no stage at the Capri, just that big wide screen.

GAFFNEY

The Star Theatre sat on the corner of North Limestone and East Birnie Streets. On Sanborn Maps for 1908 and 1926, it is shown with a long entrance off of North Limestone running past retail shops on either side. The 1926 map shows that a former piano store at 406 North Limestone had become a movie theater. This, according to several directories of the time, is likely the Strand Theater.

The Hammrick Theater at 306 North Limestone opened in 1930. It closed around 1968 and was later torn down.

The Cherokee Theater opened on November 20, 1936 at 302 North Limestone. Around 1969, the name was changed to the Capri Theater.

Clyde and Mary Hudson
Owners of Capri Theater
June 31, 2002

Mary:
"The Hamrick, just down the street, was a nice theater but it just deteriorated after movies were no longer shown. The roof started leaking. It was offered to the local community theater but the inside had gotten really bad so they didn't take it. It stayed empty for a few more years and they just tore it down."

Clyde:
"The Capri used to be the Cherokee Theatre. When the Cherokee opened it seated 500 people. It had a stage then. Many country and western singers of the time like Little Jimmy Dinkens and Ernest Tubb would put on their shows in the local movie theaters because that was the only place they had to play.

Mary, Beau and Clyde Hudson
in the lobby of the Capri Theater

One of the amazing things about this theater is that is has been run continuously since it opened in 1936. The theater was remodeled from front to back in 1969 and 1970. The city had an ordinance that said nothing could hang over the sidewalk so the marquee had to be taken down then."

Mary:
"We couldn't show movies on Sundays until sometime in the 1970's. We were the last theater in South Carolina to show movies on Sunday. Then for a long time we couldn't open until one o'clock and we had to close between five and seven because those were church hours. Eventually the bowling alleys and skating rinks applied pressure and we were able to stay open on Sundays.

Sometimes people bring their children back to see movies at the Capri. One woman came to me and asked, "Do you remember me?" I told her, "Yes, you're the one who wrote on the ladies' room wall. I gave you a roll of paper towels and a bottle of cleaner and made you clean it off." The woman said, "That was me all right."

Capri Theater - 2002

Cherokee Theater - 1940
"South of the Border" with Gene Autry

Cherokee Theater - 1961

Photographs courtesy of Clyde and Mary Hudson

Hamrick Theater - 1953

Grand Opening Tonite

Doors Open 7:30—Show Starts at 8 O'clock

One of Metro-Goldwyn-Mayer's Finest Pictures.

"LIBELED LADY"

·Starring·

Wm. Powell - Myrna Loy - Spencer Tracy - Jean Harlow

TO-NITE AND SATURDAY	Admission: Adults _____ 25c Children _____ 10c

| —SOON— "Small Town Girl" with Robt. Taylor. "PIGSKIN PARADE" The Big Football Picture. | **Cherokee** THEATRE "Gaffney's Finest", | MONDAY, and TUESDAY The Latest Big Tarzan Pic-ture— "TARZAN ESCAPES" Starring Jo Weissmuller and Maureen O'Sullivan |

Cherokee Theater - Advertisement 1936

Clyde Hudson and his son, Beau
in the projection booth of the Capri Theater
June 31, 2002

We settled into our seats and waited for the movie to begin. It comes upon the screen with a sudden burst of light and the sound of a studio theme or the roar of a lion. We accept this process without giving a thought to the person far behind and above us in a tiny hot room, making this magic happen.

Working in the typical projection booth of the single-screen movie theater, up until the 1970s, meant threading a 35 mm projector by hand. The large reels of film were heavy and fragile. The carbon arch rods that provided the light was extremely hot and had to be manually adjusted from time to time. The carbon arc was replaced by xenon lamps in the 1960s, but these were also very hot and dangerous.

A typical feature film came on several reels. When one reel was nearly finished, the next reel was started on a second projector. The first projector was threaded with the next reel and prepared to start in its turn.

Eventually reels were replaced by a single platter holding the entire feature film. Today's movie theaters are rapidly switching to digital movies stored on a computer hard drive.

Beau threading film on a 1940s era lamphouse projector

Projector's complex transport mechanism

GEORGETOWN

Airdome Theater

Opened in 1909, at 718 Front Street, by Mr. D.C. Simpkins as an open-air picture show, the Airdome Theater consisted of a platform covered in iron. In 1910 the Airdome was improved by closing in the top with a substantial roof to keep out the rain. Admission was five and ten cents.

1914 Advertisement for Airdome Theater

Electric Theater

This was a short-lived theater located at 810 Front Street. It is likely that it closed before 1915. Mr. D.C. Simpkins, who owned the Airdome at the time, also owned and operated the Electric Theater.

The Princess and the Peerless

There were actually two Princess Theaters on Front Street in Georgetown. The first opened on May 22, 1914, at 624 Front Street, under the ownership of Mr. Fritz Young, Mr. O.P. Bourke and Mr. T.W. Barfield. In November, 1914, Mr. Wilson Arnholter acquired an interest in the Princess. In August, 1915, Mr. Arnholter and Mr. L.B. Steele purchased the Princess.

In October, 1916, a fire started in the projection booth and quickly spread. The Princess Theater building burned to the ground.

Princess Theater - 624 Front Street

The Peerless Theater opened to a packed house on June 24, 1914, at 710 Front Street. It was built by Mr. Wilson B. Arnholter, who had acquired the Airdome Theater and an interest in the Princess Theater.

The Peerless Theater closed five months later in November, 1914, because there was not enough business to support three theaters. It was leased to two African American men, Mr. J.A. Baxter and Dr. S.S. Bruington, but the lease was recinded.

The theater was reopened by Mr. Arnholter on January 17, 1917. Accounts of its name at this time vary from one source to another.

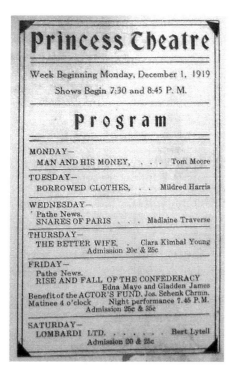

Princess Theater - 710 Front Street
1919 to 1929
Program is for December, 1919

It opened as the Princess Theater on November 15, 1919 and remained the Princess until 1928, when it was purchased by the Abrams Brothers who changed the name back to the Peerless Theater. It remained the Peerless Theater until around 1939, when it was replaced by the new Strand Theater.

Peerless Theater - 710 Front Street
1938 Program

Peerless Theatre is Damaged By Fire
Second Loss Sustained by Owners Within Few Months - Heavy Blow to Them

Saturday evening about 7 o'clock, fire was discovered in the rear portion of the Peerless Theatre on the inside of the building. The alarm was sent in and by prompt and excellent work of our fire department the fire was confined to its starting point and the beautiful little building was saved, except the rear end of the structure. It was a most difficult fire to handle and the department deserves a great deal of credit for confining the blaze to the end of the building.

The burning of the "Peerless" is a heavy blow to Mr. W. B. Arnholter, the owner. It will be remembered that only a short time ago, Messrs Arnholter and Steele purchased the "Princess" theatre and ran that show house until fire started in the operating room and destroyed the building. On the first of November the "Peerless," which had been leased to other parties, was taken over by Messrs Arnholter and Steele, who had the building put in first class condition and about two weeks ago, it was opened again for the pleasure of their patrons and large audiences were in attendance on each night's performance.

At the time during the fire great fears were entertained for the Farmers and Merchants Bank building on one side and the Barfield Printing Company building on the other side. Both these building were in close proximity to the Peerless.

Strand Theatre

The Strand Theater opened Monday, October 6, 1941, at 710 Front Street, with "Blossoms in the Dust" starring Greer Garson and Walter Pidgeon. It was built by the Abrams brothers and constructed by P.W. Munneke.

All the theaters in Georgetown closed on October 31, 1963. In January, 1964, the Strand Theater reopened under new management.

It is currently the home of the Swamp Fox Players who provide the community with an active live theatrical season. The marquee is original. The box office was built in 1987 for the movie "Made in Heaven." In December, 2011, movies returned to the Strand Theater sponsored by a group called Strand Cinema. Films will be shown when the Swamp Fox Players are not using the theater.

We are very grateful to the Georgetown County Historical Society and The Georgetown County Museum staff for most of the information that appears here. If you are in Georgetown, we highly recommend a visit to the museum at 632 Prince Street.

Both the Strand and Palace Theaters can be seen in the view of Front Street around 1942

Palace Theatre

Built in 1936 at 726 Front Street, the Palace Theatre was owned by Carroll and Morris Abrams along with their brothers Sidney and Helmer. The program shown below, provided by the Georgetown County Historical Society, is for the 1938 film "Adventures of Marco Polo" starring Gary Cooper, Basil Rathbone, and Lana Turner.

Palace Theater Program - 1938

The First Citizens Bank is now located on the former site of the Palace Theater.

GREENVILLE

Greenville had many theaters over the years. A motion picture theater directory of 1921 lists the Grand Opera House, the Bijou, Casino and Garing. Apparently, the Knights of Columbus Hall also exhibited motion pictures during this time.

An article in the *Greenville News* of February 8, 2006, states that the first "feature" film shown in Greenville, in 1904, at the old Main Street Courthouse was "The Great Train Robbery." A man present at that event was interviewed in 1954. He stated, "Women fainted, stalwart men paled, and children hiccupped hysterically."

The Bijou Theater opened in 1905, as the Unique, in the Bank of Commerce Building on the corner of Main and East Coffee streets.

D.W. Griffith's "Birth of a Nation" commanded a hefty $2 per ticket when it was shown at the Grand Opera House in 1916.

Like many cities in South Carolina's Upcountry, Greenville's theaters catered to the textile mill workers. In addition to the theaters operated by the mills, the Branwood Theater in West Greenville began showing special Saturday night films to accommodate mill workers' shift schedules.

When Cecil B. DeMille's "Ten Commandments" played Greenville in 1924, the audiences were so large, no downtown theater could hold them. Special exhibitions were scheduled at the Textile Hall.

In the early 1920s, five movie theaters lined and lit North Main Street; the Rialto at 124 N. Main, Bijou at 206 N. Main, the Garing at 215 N. Main, the Casino at 228 N. Main, and the Majestic at 316 N. Main. When you consider that the population of Greenville at that time was just over 23,000 people, you get some idea of how popular the movies had become.

The Rivoli Theater opened in February, 1925. With 750 seats, it was considered the finest theater in town. Harry Hardy was manager. Ethel Parkins was the cashier. Caroline B. Waters and Edward H. Sterling were the organists.

The Carolina opened in June that same year. It occupied the site of the former Majestic Theater. The Carolina had over 1,400 seats and boasted a $20,000 Wurlitzer organ. For some reason, the Carolina, as listed in directories after 1945, had only 500 seats. Architects for both the Rivoli and Carolina theaters were Beacham and LeGrand of Greenville.

The Great Depression of the 1930s, combined with a collapse in cotton prices, which directly affected many local residents, made it difficult for the theater managers to fill seats. Theaters turned to gimmicks to lure patrons. The Bijou Theater hired a circus "freak" who was eight feet tall to walk Main Street carrying a poster promoting the current movie. On some nights you could get a free dish with the purchase of a ticket. At one theater, you could register to win a car.

As the Great Depression slowly faded and cotton prices rebounded, ticket sales increased. This was aided by the approach of World War II, as people came for the latest newsreels, to see the developments in Europe.

After the war, ticket sales to downtown theaters were lost to the new popular drive-ins. The growth of suburban shopping malls (often with new movie theaters) put additional stress on downtown movie theaters.

Photograph courtesy of Marion Peter Holt

The Bijou was gutted by a fire in 1947 and never reopened. The Rivoli closed in 1949 but reopened later as the Fox. The Majestic and Casino theaters were closed by the 1960s. During the 1970s the Carolina and Fox closed. The Fox held out until 1978.

Downtown revitalization efforts have brought crowds back but the bright movie theater marquees and the nightly throngs of patrons lining up for tickets to the latest Hollywood movie are gone.

YOUR
RIVOLI
Is the Home Of
THE
FOREMOST
KIDDIE
KLUB

Sponsored By
FOREMOST DAIRIES

"SAMMY"
(Mrs. Elsie S. Hooper)
Program Director

EVERY SATURDAY MORNING AT 9
Greenville's Outstanding Kiddie Matinee!

FREE DIXIE DOODLES TO FIRST 50 BOYS & FIRST 50 GIRLS!
——Given By Professional Pharmacy——
BOXING—DANCING—WRESTLING—SINGING

CONTESTS   PRIZES

February Special   White House Ice Cream!
Watch For The LONE RANGER Ice Cream Cone!

Rivoli Theater - Greenville
Kiddie Klub advertiement

Fox Theater - Greenville
Formerly Rivoli

Souvenir Program

12th ANNIVERSARY
BIRTHDAY
CELEBRATION

Week Starting

October 4th, 1937

CAROLINA
THEATRE
GREENVILLE, SOUTH CAROLINA

IT'S OUR CELEBRATION—BUT
IT'S YOUR PARTY!

1925 - 1937

We are twelve years old—going on thirteen! We
point with pride to past performances, to wonderful
shows, properly presented in an attractive, comfortable theatre. We call your attention to the many
improvements of note made to the Carolina. The
beautiful new decorations, draperies and stage effect
. . . New Mirrophonic Sound . . . Projection Equipment . . . Aid for the Hard-of-Hearing . . . Refrig-
eration . . . and many other features to make your
Carolina one of the South's Finest.

But there are many more good things in store.
The coming months hold much in the way of outstanding new pictures. The physical appearance of
the Carolina will always be foremost in our thoughts
so, in the days to come, theatre-goers may always
find the Carolina presenting the finest programs
obtainable in surroundings both attractive and comfortable.

Help celebrate our Twelfth Anniversary by attending . . . you will see some exceptional shows
next week and every week, while, as always, the
Carolina strives to prove worthy of being called
"South Carolina's Finest."

DICK LASHLEY, Manager.

Carolina Theater - Greenville
12th Anniversary Souvenir Program

GREENWOOD

In 2003, we interviewed Myra Shaffer, Executive Director of the Greenwood Community Theater, who told us about the State Theater. "It was also a Jerry Lewis Theater for a time," she said. "Toward the end of its life as a movie theater it began to show X rated films. After it closed, the Greenwood Community Theater bought it."

Myra told us the theater was built as a hemp house, capable of mounting stage shows. "When we were cleaning up an area in the back of the theater, we found make-up mirrors from the days when they did movies and stage productions. The Austrian drapes are a contour curtain that was installed when the theater opened in 1934. The drapes and mechanism are too fragile now to use."

We asked if the State Theater had a balcony. Myra said, "Yes, but sometime in the 1980s, the seats were removed and the raked floor changed to flat tiers with tables so they could have dinner theater. That didn't go over so now we use the area for storage and electrical equipment."

Myra showed us the terrazzo entry floor and box office. "At one time the box office window was outside. The entrance doors have been moved toward the street so the box office is now inside. The terrazzo floor was covered with vinyl tiles. We took up those tiles and restored the terrazzo entry and the wooden floors in the theater."

The large concession stand was built about 1962 by Mr. Smart, who managed the theater at one time. He served "chilly dillys." I had never heard of a "chilly dilly" and asked her what it was. Myra explained that it was a dill pickle that was stuck down in a bucket of ice. They sold for ten cents.

State Theater in 1939

Commenting on the other theaters in Greenwood, Myra said, "The Ritz is still there but boarded up. The Carolina was just down the street from the State but has been torn down."

Myra is an energetic and dedicated professional who is very proud of the work of the Greenwood Community Theater. She is proud that the productions involve 150 to 200 children every year as well as 75 to 150 adults.

The Greenwood Community Theatre is located in the former State Theater which opened in 1934 at 110 Main Street.

GREER

We appreciate the following memories of the theatres in Greer shared with us by Don Fortner.

I worked in the theatre in 1962 and 1963. The managers I worked for were Mr. Reg Chesson, Mr. Aaron Bell, and Mr. Greene. It has been 44 years since I was last in the theatre. I remember it was part of my job to change the weekly lobby cards which contained all those wonderful black and white photos of the movie scenes. I think of all the old photo cards that I changed over the years and put in the trash. If I had kept all of those I would probably be wealthy today as there is such a demand now for any of the old artifacts from those movie days.

Photographs courtesy of Don Fortner

I also used to go with my boss, Mr. Greene, in his car, a 2 cyclinder Fiat, yep....it is a miracle that we both were able to get in it. I have never seen another since.

He would drive me to several locations around Greer where there were small ground mounted billboards that had promos for the upcoming or present movies being shown.

The posters were in several pieces and required that I mix up some kind of glue or powder and water paste in a bucket, and put the multi-piece poster on the board with a brush or a push broom. The handle of the broom would stick out the top of the car while we were driving around.

If I remember correctly, the boss stayed in the car and I did the work. As a young man of 17, I was thrilled to do it. Although I was a part-time employee, I remember working 90 hours one week. I had been promoted to Assistant Manager on weekends and got to work all week including Saturday, and come in and open the place up on Sunday afternoon.

I even was told that I could wear a tie and use the Manager's office as though it was mine. I really felt important for awhile. All my friends would come to the movie and I would leave the office door open so that they could see me behind the desk. Ah, the girls were really impressed.

I started off there as an usher, then behind the concession stand (I also remember the popcorn machine, I got enough experience operating it) then, when I became part-time assistant manager, I was told that I had to learn the entire operation from top to bottom. That was a lot of responsibility for a 17 year old, but I really enjoyed all the work. One thing though, it doesn't take long working behind the concession stand to get your fill of popcorn and Coke.

At the time all my friends would tell me how "lucky" I was to be able to do that. I also learned how to edit the incoming films with "Coming Attractions" inserts. It was called "building the show" and at the end of the run I would "tear down the show" before sending the film to the next theater in the chain.

I also became a fair projectionist using the old carbon rods burning for light in the projectors. I can still remember looking out the small hole in the wall of the projection booth to look for the "cue" marks coming up. I don't remember now how far apart the two sets of cues were, but when you saw the first one pop up, you had better be ready to switch the projectors when the second set came up. I got pretty good at that. There were times that you were unable to see the switch come up. The switch was always supposed to come at the end of a scene when the film momentarily went to black. The idea was to keep the black off of the screen.

As you can tell I have many fond memories of those years so long ago. I would really like to be able to walk into the theatre with things as they were way back then. I know this isn't going to happen but I can dream. The western star Lash Larue came once to the Grand Theater. Boy, were we kids excited! We thought he would act the same as in the movies we had seen, but he never even took his whip off his side or fired his gun.

By the way, you asked if we ever had any special promotions. Well, before I went to work there, I remember having onstage an Elvis impersonator contest to promote Love Me Tender. The contestants would get up on the stage and perform to 45 records ("What were those?," my grandchildren ask today.) If I remember correctly, a female dressed as Elvis won the contest. The prize was a book of free tickets worth today about $2.50.

It was so much fun and I knew someday I wanted to work at the theater. Also the theater was called the "show" as in "Let's go to the show." Very few kids called it "the movie." There was also a drive-in theatre in Greer. The marquee is still in existence. I was assistant manager at the King Cotton Drive-in in Greer.

State Representative Bob Leach shared his memories with us. We briefly interviewed SC State Representative Bob Leach in July, 2005. He recalled that when he was a young boy his aunt would give him 25 cents for the movies. He walked to Greer, saw a movie, and had money left to buy a pint of ice cream. "In 1941 and 1942, Greer had two movie theaters," he told us. "There was the Grand and the Rialto. I worked in the theater making popcorn when I was a youngster."

Hampton

From the *Hampton County Guardian*
August 14, 1946

> ## Palmetto Theatre Opened Monday Night With Capacity Crowd In Attendance

The $45,000 Palmetto Theatre opened Monday night at 8 o'clock with every seat occupied and additional chairs lining the aisle.

An estimated crowd of some 550 persons were present for the first show and to hear the welcome address by Senator George Warren who praised T. G. Stanley and Dr. J. A. Hayne for bringing to Hampton the handsome, modern, Palmetto theatre. He said further that he could recall no building project that had such unanimous approval as did this theatre for Hampton, which never before has had the privilege of a movie house.

The theater was built by C. L. Freeman, contractor. Taking care of the mechanical department is Frank McClure, Jr. and Abe Goethe. In the box office is Mrs. Irene DeLoach.

Theater Owners Arrested for Showing Movies on Sunday

In September, 1950, during a showing of the movie "Wake Island," Mr. Stanley and Dr. Hayne were arrested for showing a movie on Sunday. Mayor J.L. Holland paid $100 bond for each man. The Blue Laws of the time prohibited delivery of newspapers, operation of trains, drug stores, swimming pools and service stations on Sundays.

Dr. J.A. Hayne   T.G. Stanley

Palmetto Theatre
108 Lee Avenue

After some years in operation, T.J. "Mutt" Stanley sold his interest in the Palmetto Theatre to Dr. Hayne. Then, Bob Saxton purchased the theater and leased it to Nolan Mole. Mr. Mole closed the Palmetto Theatre in 1985. When the Hampton County Arts Council was formed in 1989, a lease-purchase agreement was reached with the Herbert J. Cooper family, who owned the theater at that time. After four years of fund raising and restoration efforts, the Palmetto Theatre opened again on September 14, 1993. It continues to serve Hampton and the surrounding area as a venue for concerts and live performances.

HARTSVILLE

Wilmont Berry recalls the Theatres in Hartsville
March 30, 2005

When we moved here to Hartsville I think they were still showing movies at the old Temple Theater. The Temple Theater was built as an auditorium and meeting place. Pretty soon they put a screen up on the stage and

Wilmont Berry

started showing movies. Teenage boys would sit in the balcony. They bought bags of peanuts to throw at the rats. Of course, that's just what the rats wanted.

After the theater closed there was a vegetable market just inside. The rest of the theater was getting pretty dilapidated. Pigeons got in there and the roof was about to cave in. When I was the building official for the City I asked the man who bought the three buildings that included the theater to do something with it. It was right in the middle of town. It was where the Centennial Park is now. It faced 5th Street.

I met him there one day and we went inside. He said he thought the building was sound. We got about half way into the theater when the floor gave way and he fell through. All that was sticking up above the floor was his head. He said, "Yeah. I reckon we ought to tear it down."

The Center Theater was built in 1935 with WPA labor. It was built for performing arts. It had a flyloft. The town had to pay part of the cost. So,

they set up a township and these people that lived about five miles around Hartsville paid a little bit of tax. That was paid off in 1967, I believe. When they built it they had some footlights but no lighting as we know it today. They had no dressing rooms.

Just before the Second World War we had some people here who wanted to do some live theater. They got started but then the war came along and stopped it. All during the war years and up until we came here in 1959, it was a movie theater. There was a screen up on the stage about six feet behind the main drape. During that time the seats were slashed. There was gum on the floor. It was pretty torn up.

W.W. Tisdale, he's a good old fellow, I think the world of him. He was the choral leader at school. Each spring he would put on a play. I got started early on helping him with them. I had a float building company in Saluda and we brought that here with us. For that reason, he asked me to help him build scenery and rigging for the lights. We did "Oklahoma" and Mr. Tisdale did all the music on a portable organ.

About 1965, the theater was a mess, and the mayor and some other people got interested in restoring the theater for live performances. During that time, the man who presented the movies in there built the Berry Theater. The community raised $200,000 and we put dressing rooms in the back, stage rigging, and lighting. We built a thrust stage to cover the orchestra pit when it was needed. The drape that is hanging in there now is the original drape that was placed in there in 1935.

We had a restored theater but nobody to use it. So, I called a few people that might be interested and asked them to meet me at the theater. They were interested and so we decided to have a community-wide meeting. We advertised the meeting and a bunch of people showed up. We set up a steering committee and got things underway. I was president of it for about ten years.

We did "Don't Drink the Water." I remember it so well. It was a nice little play and it was successful. Today the Hartsville Community Players are still going strong. The young woman who is directing the upcoming play was there from the beginning. She took part in everything we did.

This is all in that book I wrote about Hartsville. "Scraps of History: Hartsville, S.C., 1950-2003"

Temple Theater in Hartsville

Berry Theater in Hartsville - 2007

Above: Men's and Women's restroom signs in Berry Theater with dolls placed above.

Center Theater in Hartsville - 1938

HEMINGWAY

We visited Hemingway in September, 2004. We met Barbara and Teresa, who were working in the jewelry store that occupied the old Anderson Theater building. They introduced us to Brenda Player who owns the building. Brenda provided a newspaper article by Mona Burris Dukes which appeared in *The Weekly Observer* on October 7, 1982. The following information is extracted from that article.

Many residents of the area have fond memories of the old Anderson Theater. Many of these memories are brought back as they pass by the building in the process of being remodeled and see its insides again for the first time in years.

Comments around town about "good times" in the old movie theater have been on the lips of many, both young and old. Everyone has a tale to tell about what they saw there and how they used to spend Saturdays in the theater for the matinees. Many even admit shyly to courting on the back rows.

What isn't as widely known is the history of the building and the theater business.

That's where the original owners and workers come into the picture.

Harry Anderson, a long-time resident of the area, and his wife Sadie ran the theater from 1942 to the early 1960s, when they sold it to Jerry Jowers of Hemingway. Prior to that time, Anderson's brother, Hubert Anderson, had built and operated it for some two years.

According to Mrs. Anderson and former cashier Sara Hemingway, the theater was a social gathering place. People came and brought their families. Some even came with tiny babies in wicker baskets, while many of the patrons were elderly people who came to the movies for an outing.

Back in the 1940s, Mrs. Anderson recalls, couples would come to the shows on a regular basis. She and Mrs. Hemingway remember many names of those who attended and wonder what became of many of them.

Mrs. Hemingway, who worked at the theater for $8 a week, can reel off the names of local men who worked as concessions boys and ticket takers during her long stint as cashier. "I worked there 32 and a half years," she recalls. "That's how I got to know so many people."

The crowds were good for shows all week long, according to Mrs. Anderson and Mrs. Hemingway. Unlike now, when so many people wait for the weekend to see a movie, the theater would have good patronage nightly.

"We usually showed a show on Monday and Tuesday, a different show on Wednesday, and another one on Thursday and Friday," Mrs. Anderson recalls. Saturdays were reserved for western and cartoon matinees, and there was a late show on Saturday evenings.

Mrs. Hemingway remembers when the line formed for the late show all the way around the corner. She says people came from miles around to see a movie, which was the only one around after Chives Prosser closed the old theater in Johnsonville.

When the Andersons first took over the theater, admission for children was nine cents, while adults had to pay around 25 cents. Mrs. Anderson recalls thinking it was outrageous when they charged $1 for patrons to see the classic hit "Gone With The Wind."

When asked what the longest running movie was during his theater ownership, Anderson replies that "Thunder In Carolina" a movie filmed in Darlington starring Robert Mitchum played for one whole week.

As far as the layout of the theater is concerned, the Andersons and Mrs. Hemingway recall approximately 300 seats downstairs and 200 in the balcony area. There was a projection room and a "paper room" where flyers and advertisements were kept and organized.

The lobby consisted of the box office and a concession area, as well as a display area for coming attractions.

Several live performances were given at the theater, including special appearances by movie greats Gabby Hayes and Lash Larue. The platform in front of the screen served as a stage for the performers.

Harry Anderson would saunter through the aisles at random, and if he caught anyone misbehaving, he would banish them from the movies for several weeks – certain agony for children who knew no other Saturday entertainment.

One such reprimand was given to Charlie McElveen, who later worked as projectionist for Anderson. McElveen was asked to leave the theater after propping his feet on the back of a chair during a particularly frightening part of a horror movie.

Jimmy Chinnes recalls many days spent watching the good old westerns and monster movies. He even remembers when 3-D movies would be shown. A busboy was sent from the A&J Restaurant on some Saturdays to bring hot dogs to the kids who had had their fill of popcorn and soda.

An Andrews resident rented the theater for several years, during which time he resorted to showing martial arts movies and, eventually, x-rated shows. Mrs. Hemingway declares that, though she continued to work as cashier "out of necessity" she never saw an x-rated movie. "As soon as my work in the box office was done, I would go home," she confirms.

The crowds came for a time, but soon the enthusiasm died down and the quality of the patrons diminished. After the Andersons sold the building to Jowers, no more movies were shown.

Gerald Player has owned the theater building for approximately nine months and was forced to either fix such flaws as the leaky roof or let the building deteriorate into a condemned state.

He plans to redo the inside, replacing all old lumber and roofing, and will add a store front where the old lobby used to be.

HONEA PATH

We stopped for lunch at John's Place in Honea Path, a small town located between Laurens and Anderson, South Carolina. We were served large portions of southern cooking. The prices were low and included a meat, two vegetables, a biscuit, cold iced tea and dessert. "Who are you and why are you here?" asked the older gentleman in the booth across the aisle. The questions were direct but not unfriendly.

Mark smiled and replied to the man in the booth. He introduced us and explained that we were researching the history of movie theaters in South Carolina. The man responded, "I'm Gerald Bratcher. I lived out in the country and we didn't see many movies." He smiled. "When I was little movies around here and in Anderson and Belton were charging a dime to get in. Then they passed a law that you had to charge a seat tax on anything over a dime, so they cut the price to nine cents. Up to twelve years old you could get in on a child's ticket. I remember walking up and squatting down. People didn't have much money and they'd rather have our dime than nothing."

"In Anderson at the old Criterion Theater that had a stage they would have some live shows. I can remember seeing Johnnie and Jack when they were first starting. And, another thing, they had a movie, I assume about Dillinger, and they displayed the car that he was in when he got shot. They had it on a trailer and parked it in front of the theater. It impressed us little kids."

Gerald didn't recall the first movie he saw, but he did remember that it was in Newport News, Virginia in 1943. He had gone with the family to see his older brother go off to World War II. After the brother left, his parents took him to a movie.

"I do remember as a young boy watching one movie over and over. There was a scene where some women were going swimming. Just as they were getting undressed, a train came by. We started yelling, "Get out of the way! Get out of the way!" When the train passed, the women were already in the water. We watched that movie three times. My friend said he'd never known a train yet that was always on time."

After lunch Gerald walked outside with us. He told us the Lyric Theater in Honea Path was diagonally across the street from John's Place. "The Lyric is gone now." he said.

Photograph courtesy of Gerald Bratcher

Lyric Theater photograph from the 1957 Honea Path High School yearbook. The young man in the white sport coat is Gerald Bratcher.

KINGSTREE

Alice Eatmon recalls the
Anderson Theatre in Kingstree
March 29, 2005

In my younger years we went to the movies every Saturday. My mother worked here in town. My uncle would drop me and my two older sisters off at the movies. We would go to a double header that started about two o'clock. You would get out about seven-thirty. That cost ten cents. We would sit through two Westerns.

One Saturday a movie star, Lash LaRue came to town. He was the one with the whip. He had eight-by-ten black and white photographs. You went down and he would autograph them and give them to you. He had to give them to us because none of us had any money.

When I was in high school, Edward and I would walk downtown to the movies. There wasn't any crime and we didn't worry about anything. Sometimes groups of us would walk together down to the movies. Edward's mother was married to a judge who was out of town on Monday, Wednesday, and Friday. When he was gone, she would go to the matinees in the afternoon. They had those wonderful movies. Nothing like they have today.

When you walked up to the ticket booth you bought your ticket from Mrs. Tisdale. She had red hair and a good looking figure, and was so friendly. Then you'd go into the lobby. The floor was little black and white tiles. And right in front of you was

Alice and Edward Eatmon - 1950s

Jim Owens. We called him James Watson and he was in charge of making the popcorn and all that.

On the left was a bathroom for the men and on the right there was one for the women. Then you went into the theater and walked down the aisle to your seat. It had a center row of seats and then seats on each side.

After Ed and I got married we'd go to the nine o'clock movie at night and then (she smiled) and all that stuff. There was a wonderful doctor here in town, Dr. James Claffy Montgomery. He would come in with his two youngest children. One would be in his arms with a football helmet on. He was two or three years old. He would fall asleep with his head over his daddy's shoulder. That was probably the only time of day the doctor had with his children.

Anderson Theater - Kingstree - 1953

Program for May 16 - 21, 1949

We loved to watch them come in. The little one always sat in his daddy's lap and fell asleep. They were well behaved. You know back then we didn't move around. We sat still.

Cartoons came on first, like Looney Tunes' Bugs Bunny. We had the sing-alongs with the white bouncing ball. You know the 1950s, after the war, was the greatest time. The war was so awful. I remember after the war, I was about six, my mother said there were two things she was going to have done. We lived about four miles out of town on the Charleston highway. The house had never been painted. She was going to have that house painted inside and out. And, she was going to have a car.

The first thing they did was buy a four-door, navy blue Chevrolet from Manning, South Carolina for nine hundred dollars. That car and having the house painted really made them happy. Today, that would be nothing to most folks.

I remember when "Gone With The Wind" showed in a movie theater in Charleston. My mother went with a bunch of other women from Kingstree. I stayed with my grandmother. She said that when Rhett Butler said, "Frankly my dear, I don't give a damn," everyone in the audience gasped.

The 1945 edition of *Film Daily Yearbook* lists the Anderson Theater of Kingstree with 400 seats.

On January 7, 1968, the newspaper carried a notice stating that Cinemas Unlimited had acquired the Anderson Theater and it would now be called the Kingstree Cinema.

On February 18, 1968, the Anderson Theater burned. The fire is thought to have started in the projection room. The building was completely destroyed.

Lake City

Early in 1916 two movie theatres opened in Lake City, the Idle Hour Motion Picture Company and the New Theatre. That autumn F.W. Rutledge moved his Idle Hour into the 1,000-seat McClam Theatre, newly constructed by J. S. McClam.

Located midway on the north side of West Main Street's first block, its air was cooled by electric fans and recirculated every five minutes.

The New Theatre closed its doors forever after the opening of the state-of-the-art McClam. Louie L. Propst, Sr. and W. A. McClam bought the McClam in 1931 and changed its name to the Ritz.

In 1950 Louie L. Propst Sr. built and opened the Propst Theatre next door to the corner Esso gasoline station. For the next six years, Lake City had two in-door theatres one block apart, the Ritz and the Propst, each running a matinee and an evening show daily, except Sundays.

The Ritz Theatre closed in 1956. In 1969 the Propst Theatre closed and was immediately razed to make way for a new shopping center, called the Lake City Plaza.

Kent and Carol Daniels on the Propst Theater

Growing up in Lake City in the mid-twentieth century was like growing up in Paradise. Most neighborhoods had tree houses, jungles, secret meeting places, and loads of children roaming at will. Life was full of fun, but by far, everyone's favorite form of fun was going to the show at the Propst Theatre on Saturday afternoons.

The theater's main entrance was below the large marquee. The ticket booth was to the left. We were aware of the small round window in the top center, because the projectionist sometimes stuck his head out to escape the heat.

The Propst Theatre (1947-1969)
Photo courtesy of Wayne and Ronnie McKnight

The cost of admission was 25 cents per child and for an additional 25 cents, you could feel like a king or queen. For that extra 25 cents you could buy a Coca-Cola, popcorn, and candy, which would last the entire time you were there. The movies at the Propst started at noon on Saturdays and had either a double feature (two full-length movies) or occasionally a triple feature.

You entered a different world when you stepped into the Propst. At movie time, the beautiful art deco side lights went down and the crimson curtain opened. First up were the coming attractions, followed either by a newsreel or serial, then a cartoon or two. Finally the first feature movie began, immediately followed by the second feature. For that quarter's admission, you stayed and watched for as long as you liked, or rather, until your parents picked you up or you had to walk home before dark. Those were some of the happiest days of our youth.

Theater Pass - 1951

Ritz Theater - around 1941

   Photo courtesy of Sam Mac Propst
and Charles M. Dalziel

Ritz Theater - 2005

   Some of the Ritz Theatre remains on
Main Street. The skeletal structure has been
retained. We took a photograph of the
"bones" of the old theatre in 2005.

Ritz Theater - 2008

   We returned to Lake City in 2008 and
discovered that the former Ritz Theater
property has been beautifully reclaimed as
a public park behind a restored facade. This
is a most creative use of a former movie
theater site. It retains an architectural
reference to the site's historic purpose while
providing a unique and contemporary use
for the community.

LAURENS

The Idle Hour, at 107 East Laurens, was listed in the 1917 Laurens City Directory. At that time, A.S. Perry is listed as the manager.

The sign promotes a "Bale of Cotton Given Away" to the one with the most votes. Each ten cent ticket was worth ten votes, each five cent ticket was worth five votes.

Idle Hour on the north side of the square

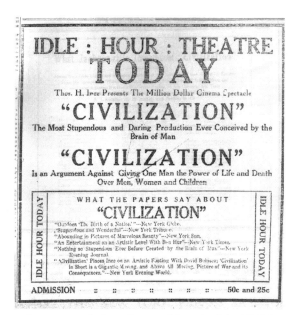

Laurens Advertiser - March 14, 1917

Gus Mason

Mr. Gus Mason opened the Capitol Theater in Laurens on June 10, 1926. In 1974, Mr. Mason recalled, "The initial receipts were poor and rather depressing, but business picked up as months passed by. Then the depression hit, and attendance was really off. After the banks re-opened and the mills began production again, people started going to the movies more and more."

During World War II, business increased. Mr. Mason opened a second movie theater in Laurens, the Echo Theater. Each theater had two showings in the afternoon and two in the evening. Every morning there was a showing at one of the theaters for the people working on certain shifts at the local mills.

The popularity of Drive-Ins and the introduction of television caused attendance to fall off at the Laurens movie houses. Mr. Mason said, "Up until the time that I retired from the motion picture business in 1963, the crowds got smaller and smaller."

A.I. "Gus" Mason

Capitol Theater - 1958

In 1964 the Capitol Theater closed its doors. Then in the late 1990's, Ronnie and Debbie Campbell purchased the building to open a ladies clothing store.

After discovering the historic stage and theater in workable condition, Ronnie was bitten by the renovation bug. He began the arduous task of renovating the Capitol Theater and bringing new life to a grand old building.

In 2004, Ronnie and Debbie opened the Capitol Cafe in the front of the building. Then in October 2006, Ronnie installed a new marquee reminiscent of the original sign for the theater. Finally, in May 2007, Ronnie and Debbie opened the theater to first run movies.

Capitol Theater - 2008

Echo Theater about 1966

LORIS

The Horry Herald
Thursday, August 5, 1937

Loris Theatre Opens Monday

The new State Theatre in Loris will have its grand opening Monday night, August 9th when the doors will open at 7 P.M. The people living along the border of the two states can justly feel proud of their "community" theatre as it can be truly said that it is one of the most modern theatres to be found in either of the Carolinas. No expense has been spared to make this one of the entertainment centers for the people in the community which the theatre will serve. Mr. J.C. Thompson, the lessee, a young experienced theatre operator, made the following statement: "We decided to locate our theatre in Loris because we felt that we were more in the center of the people in the community which we expect to serve. It will be our policy to give our people the very best in movie entertainment under the most comfortable conditions. With their support and patronage they may expect pictures and programs that will equal the best to be found anywhere in the country."

The State Theatre will have international spring cushion seats, RCA high fidelity sound, supreme ventilating equipment, the latest projection machines and other equipment and features found in the larger city theatres. The floor plan was drawn by a foremost authority on theatre seating with the idea of giving the utmost in comfort and vision. The front will be beautifully illuminated with neon lights especially designed for this theatre.

Mr. J.J. Sanderson will be the manager of the new house. Mr. Forrest Humphrey will be in charge of projection, and Miss Nell Hughes will be the cashier.

A gala program has been planned for the opening week with brand new pictures. In some instances the pictures will represent first showing in the Carolinas. A complete opening week program will be found elsewhere in this paper.

MANNING

The earliest movie theater we can find in Manning was the Pastime Theater located at 31 N. Brooks Street. It was a combination house offering live shows and movies. The 1927 edition of *Film Yearbook* lists the theater with 300 seats. A Sanborn Map of 1921 shows the theater on N. Brooks Street noting its use as "Movies." The map does not indicate the name of the theater. Manning had a population of 2,025 at the time.

In an article in *The Manning Times* dated January 24, 1917, it is noted:

> J.E. King & Co., of Sumter, agents for The Edison Re-Creation Machine have placed two of their machines in the Pastime Theater and the patrons of this theater have a rare musical treat ahead of them. This machine has stood the most rigid tests imaginable and it brings out Edison's ambition for many years to create a machine that would make the voice perfectly natural. The Re-Creation is the rusult. Go hear it tonight.

In 1922, Pastime Theater presented Kamaka's Native Hawaiians. This live vaudeville show was followed by the movie "The Right That Failed." The program ran for only one day with a matinee and two evening performances. Adults price was 60 cents, children 30 cents.

By 1938, we no longer find any mention of the Pastime Theater. But, we do find the Hollywood Theater listed in several issues of *The Manning Times*. On a trip to Manning in 2005, we met the owner of Mike's Grill and Deli, who told us there had been a movie theater on the second floor of the building across the street. That is the corner of West Boyce and South Brooks Streets. Janet Meleney, the archivist at the Clarendon County Archives, recalled it as "Mrs. Green's Theater."

"The Right That Failed" - 1922
Metro Pictures - Silent Film

Film Daily Yearbook for 1945 lists the Hollywood Theater, and a newspaper article from 1985, mentions, in its "Looking Back" column, that the Hollywood Theater in 1945, was showing "Law of the Valley" starring Johnny Mack Brown and Raymond Hatton. We suspect, but haven't confirmed that "Mrs. Green's Theater" was the Hollywood Theater.

Hollywood Theatre

Manning, S. C.

NIGHT SHOW STARTS 7:45 P. M.

THURSDAY — FRIDAY

JULY 14-15

Matinee Thursday 3:30 P. M.

"HER JUNGLE LOVE"

With Dorothy Lamour and Ray Milland

Also Comedy and News

Friday—Chapter 10 of

"LONE RANGER"

SATURDAY

JULY 16

Show Start 3 P. M.

GENE AUTRY in

Springtime in the Rockies

Also Comedy and Chapter 10 of

"LONE RANGER"

MONDAY - TUESDAY

JULY 18-19

Matinee Monday 3:30 P. M.

Special—Championship Fight Between Joe Louis and Max Schmeling

In Slow Motion

ALSO

"Cocoanut Gaove"

With Fred McMurray and Harriet Hillard

Also Comedy and News

WEDNESDAY

JULY 20

Matinee 3:30 P. M.

"Assassin Of Youth"

Also Comedy

Hollywood Theater Schedule
January 13, 1938

On that trip in 2005, we interviewed Nelson Parker, who told us, "My father was Leighton Brown Parker and my mother was Nelson Hill before she married my father. The theater was named Parkhill, combining my parents' names.

I'm not sure when the theater was constructed, but it was during a time when bricks were being rationed. I think it was toward the end of the Second World War. Somehow, my father and my grandfather were able to acquire the brick to construct the theater.

My mother operated the ticket booth. We all worked there including me and my brothers, Brownie and Hill. We all made popcorn and helped in the concession stand. I remember that when the film "Doctor Zhivago" played at the Parkhill, we all wore little Cossack hats.

A black man named Wesley Billups, ran the projectors. He had a mustache. I called him "Zorro" because he looked like the guy who played "Zorro" on T.V. Wesley was, to my mother and father, one of the most honorable men that my family has ever known. He was an extraordinary guy and like a member of our family.

We had a dog named Spotwoods who was the son of a circus dog. The theater was within walking distance of our home and Spotwoods would follow us and then sit and wait outside for us to leave. Then he would follow us home. If it was raining, Spotwoods would jump into Wesley's truck and wait for him to drive him home.

I remember that actors who were in the films would sometimes come to the theater. Movie stars, you know, minor screen stars would accompany the film to generate publicity. My sister, Sherry, recalled that when one of the Tarzan movies was playing, someone showed up with the chimp that was in the movie. The chimp created a real ruckus with the kids.

When the Beatles' movie "A Hard Days Night" came out, my family was running the theater. But, when the second Beatles' movie "Help" was shown, Lewis Watkins was running the theater. Before the show, Lewis Watkins, who was in his sixties, stood up in front of the theater and introduced the film as if he was introducing the Beatles to everybody. He wanted everyone to know the significance of this band. It was a fun time.

Photograph courtesy Larry Hewett, Silver Images Photographic, Manning, SC

My parents operated the theater until about 1966 or 1967. Around that time it was leased to Lewis Watkins and his son Michael. When they took over operation of the Parkhill Theater, they dressed up the front a little bit and added the ironwork."

When we showed Nelson Parker a photograph of the theater we had obtained from local photographer, Larry Hewett, he grinned. "That's my class!" he said. "The man in the suit and glasses is Reverend Haynes. He was the minister at the First Baptist Church here in Manning and was Headmaster of what was then called The Christian Academy. This photograph is of a special afternoon showing of 'The Ten Commandments' for The Christian Academy." He pointed out several people and named them.

PARKHILL THEATRE

MATINEE DAILY 3:30 — NIGHT 7:30 and 9:15

SATURDAY — Continuous from 1:30
"AIR CONDITIONED"

PROGRAM WEEK OF AUG. 26 TO SEPT. 9TH

Thursday and Friday
"FEUDIN' FUSSIN' and FIGHTING"
—Starring—
Donald O'Connor • Marjorie Main • Percy Kilbride
—Don't Miss Seeing This One—

Saturday (Double Feature)
"DESPERATE TRAIL"
Johnnie Mack Brown • Fuzzy Knight • Bob Baker
—Also—
"BLONDIES ANNIVERSARY"
Penny Singleton • Arthur Lake • Larry Simms

Monday and Tuesday
"Abbott and Costello Meet Frankenstein"
Starring
Bud Abbott • Lou Costello • Lon Chaney
—It's a Grand Idea for Fun—

Wednesday
"MATING OF MILLIE"
Glenn Ford • Evelyn Keyes • Ron Randell

Parkhill Theater Schedule
August 4, 1948

MARION

An article in 1892 in the newspaper, the *Morning Star*, regarding the opening of the new Opera House, stated, "…it is hoped there will no longer be 'dread monotony of crushing calm' in Marion."

The 1914 *Cahn Hill Directory* lists the Opera House with Mr. O.K. La Roque, manager. People coming to Marion for a performance could stay at the Carmichael or Park View Hotel for $2 per day.

By 1920, the Opera House was no longer in use and was sold to Marion Motor Company. The city purchased the building in 1997 when the automobile dealership closed. Today, it houses a 300-seat auditorium used by the *Mullins Playmakers* theater group, various community and civic organizations, and the Marion Chamber of Commerce. It is located on the corner of Main and Godbold Streets.

In the 1920s, Marion had two movie theaters. The Colored, seating 300, and The Idle Hour, seating 500. Both theaters were managed by Mr. D.K. Davis. The 1927 edition of the *Film Yearbook* lists the Rainbow Theater in Marion. It was located at 307 N. Main Street.

Rainbow Theater in 1970 - Marion

The Rainbow Theater was more than a place to show the latest films from Hollywood. It was part of the fabric of the community. It provided baby-sitting services so mothers could go shopping on Saturday. It also provided information that we now find on cable television or the internet. One such example is "Star In My Kitchen" a film which was exhibited at the Rainbow Theatre, October 13, 14, and 15, 1938.

This one-hour and fifty-minute film was promoted as a "Motion Picture Cooking School" by *The Enterprise* newspaper in Mullins. "Lock the doors and come to town!" prompted a page-one story on Thursday, October 6, 1938. The article described the event as "entirely free to every woman in town."

In addition to the film, there were cooking demonstrations, model kitchens, recipe sheets, and gifts. Women were encouraged to "hear the informal chats from one-good-cook-to-another." The film was also exhibited in Mullins.

The schedule of events at the Rainbow Theatre for the week of January 30, through February 3, 1945, is a good example of the typical fare available in most of the single-screen movie theaters at the time. Wednesday's movie was "Girl of the Big House" with Lynn Roberts and Richard Powers, followed by Chapter 5 of the twelve-part serial "Federal Operator." Wednesday night's were "Cash Night" at the Rainbow Theatre.

"Cash Night," was a promotion used to get patrons into the theater on nights when attendance was traditionally low. Prizes were usually $100. If no one claimed the prize, it was increased to $150 and the drawing repeated the following week. This promotion helped the manager fill the theater on off nights and allowed him to run cheap films to a packed house.

The movie for Thursday and Friday was "What Next, Corporal Hargrove?" with Robert Walker and Keenan Wynn. These nights included a "News" film. During World War II, the only place to see moving pictures of the war was in the local movie theater's news reels.

Saturday the Rainbow Theater exhibited "Marshall of Laredo" with Wild Bill Elliott as Red Ryder and Robert Blake as Little Beaver, followed by Chapter 4 of "Jungle Raiders." This was a fifteen-part serial. The plot revolves around a doctor who has discovered the "miracle drug" of the century, but who has vanished in the jungle and may be a prisoner in a lost city! The dangers faced by our hero included a pit filled with daggers, a crocodile infested river, and molten lava.

There was an "Owl Show" on Saturday night that started at 10:00 p.m. This show was "Voice of the Whistler," the fourth film of the Columbia Studio's series based on the CBS radio program. "The Whistler" starred Richard Dix and Lynn Merrick. This movie was followed by a cartoon.

Monday and Tuesday, the theater offered "Doll Face" with Vivian Blaine and Carmen Miranda followed by a "News" program.

There was a special "Late Show" on Monday night which was billed as a "Mystery motion picture" followed by a live stage show called "Zombies Jamboree" with "World Celebrated Magician Mystic Shore" in person. It was advertised as "Ghastly, Horrific, and Out of This World." It couldn't have been too horrific as children got in at a reduced price. Admission for this special evening was fifty cents for adults and thirty cents for children under twelve.

SPECIAL LATE SHOW 10.00 P. M.
RAINBOW THEATRE
Monday, February 4
ADMISSION: Under 12, 30¢;   Adults 50¢

We interviewed several residents of Marion in 2005. Patsy Ammons recalled, "My aunt Delle Smith worked at the Rainbow Theatre. I had to be real good when I went to the theater because she was working there. I remember the cowboy movies. The theater had a balcony and I think it had a stage."

Two men at the local hardware store also remembered the Rainbow Theater and the simpler times. One of them told us, "We rode our bicycles to the theatre and parked them in the bike rack on the street in front of the theater. We didn't worry about anybody stealing them. I went a few times to see Lash LaRue and the cowboy movies. I remember how sticky the floor was. People spilled their drinks and your feet would stick to the floor."

By the mid-1950's two drive-ins were operating in the area. Competing with the Rainbow Theater was the Swamp Fox Drive-In in Marion, and the Mullins 76 Drive-In. But, otherwise, not much had changed. The Rainbow was still showing the same feature on Monday and Tuesday, a fresh title on

Wednesday, another film on Thursday and Friday and a western on Saturday. An advertisement in the *Marion Star* of November 7, 1955, listed "Apache Ambush" followed by Chapter 12 of the "Batman" serial and a cartoon. Television was beginning to draw audiences away from the local movie theaters.

Dallis Brady, who owns the popular restaurant "Dallis Downtown" told us, "I remember going to the Rainbow Theatre. You could get in for fifteen cents. For a quarter you could get popcorn, a drink, and Goobers. I loved it and I can remember being so sad when they closed it."

Around 1970, the Rainbow Theater closed. It soon reopened as the Marion Theatre. Now, one film would be shown for three or four days. Double features were often shown. Television continued to pull more customers away from the theaters. In an advertisement in the spring of 1971, a marketing phrase hinted at the changing times, "Bring the Family Life Back… See a Movie Together."

Hollywood was competing with television and losing. Lower attendance meant smaller profits. Much needed theater improvements and repairs were put off. Eventually, the Marion Theater just couldn't compete with the multiplex.

The old theater building at 307 N. Main Street was bought by Carolina Power and Light. Then, Marion National Bank bought it and built a new bank on the property. It is now Carolina First Bank."

November 7, 1955

April 12, 1971

Mount Pleasant

Going to the movies in Mount Pleasant meant going to either the Parkway Theater or the Seabreeze Drive-In. Both were located on what is now Coleman Boulevard. At the time the road was known as King's Highway.

Mr. Sidney Query (1920-1991) opened the Parkway Theater in October, 1951. It closed around 1954.

We spoke with Jimmy Lowe at Belva's Flower Shop in Mount Pleasant on Septemeber 14, 2007. He remembered the Parkway Theater. "We enjoyed The Durango Kid, Flash Gordon, and Hoot Gibson," he recalled.

News & Courier - January 3, 1953

Note: The Serial being shown at the Saturday matinee was "Nyoka & The Tiger Men" which was originally made in 1942 as "Perils of Nyoka" and re-released in 1952. The matinee cowboy feature was not "Texas Trail" but "The Old Texas Trail" with Rod Cameron which was released in 1944.

EVENING FEATURE

"Dream Boat" was released in 1952

MYRTLE BEACH

Gloria Theater

The Gloria Theater was built around 1937. It was located near Myrtle Beach's famous Pavillion at 210 9th Avenue North. The name changed in the early 1970s to the Fox Theater.

Rivoli Theater in 2009

Rivoli Theater
908 Chester Street
Opened: June 19, 1958

The Rivoli Theater opened at 908 Chester Street on June 19, 1958. Costing $400,066, the theatre was designed by architect Harold J. Riddle and built by Crescent Beach contractor J.A. Baldwin.

With 1,078 seats, including a stadium-seating style balcony, the Rivoli boasted the latest in a four-channel stereophonic sound system. Its screen measured 21 X 50 feet. The lobby featured terrazzo floors and walnut paneling. Of four other theaters in Myrtle Beach, the Rivoli alone featured a full-service refreshment stand.

The theater has been used as a children's theater and then as a nightclub.

In 1999, the City of Myrtle Beach purchased the property for around $700,000 with intent to convert it to a 500-seat performing arts center, primarily as a venue for the many non-profit performing arts groups in the community.

Broadway Theater in 2009

Broadway Theater
The Broadway Theater opened in the 1940s at 811 Main Street. It was known for a time as the Cinema Theater. It is now a retail shop.

Camelot Theater
The Camelot Theater at 1901 Kings Highway North opened in 1967 as a single-screen theater. It was divided into a twin around 1975 and soon became a three-screen theater. In closed in 1990.

Newberry

Memories of the Ritz Theater

Jane Britt, a resident of Newberry, took us into the Ritz Theater and gave us a tour.

"I left Newberry when I was twenty, but I remember the gift shop on the side of the theater because I registered my silver and china there."

Jane took us into the auditorium. We stood in the dark while she turned on the lights. With a click, the auditorium was illuminated by Art Deco sconces running the length of the room on either side.

"I told you it would take your breath away. I get such enjoyment out of showing this to people. I get chilly bumps. They are the original fixtures. I think that's the original carpet too. The theater is 8,610 square feet.

We had 517 little kids in here recently for a children's performance of "Annie." We had about 10 seats left empty. When you stand in the front of the theater it just looks like an ocean of seats.

The pit was there when I was a child but we covered it up because somebody fell in and broke a leg. There are four sconce lights in the balcony but we turned them off since we don't use the balcony for seating. There is a separate outside entrance to the balcony which was used by blacks in earlier times. Unlike the padded seats downstairs, the balcony seats are plain wood.

The projection equipment is all gone but it still has the fireproof doors in case there was a fire in the projection booth.

They did an architectural survey of Newberry in 1979 and the Ritz was not designated as historic because it wasn't fifty years old at the time. But, a young ambitious fellow who works for the city of Newberry has all the materials I took to him. He's trying to get us listed on the National Historic Registry. We want to preserve the Art Deco theater. We have an architectural board of review here and I'm sure there won't be any drastic changes to the exterior of the building."

Ritz Theater - 2002

Original Art Deco Sconce Light

ORANGEBURG

Orangeburg has had a variety of "brick and mortar" theaters as well as tent shows and some interesting "traveling" theaters.

An interesting traveling show came to the Carolina Theatre in April, 1936. The Chilean Nitrate Educational Bureau, Inc., in cooperation with all fertilizer distributors of Orangeburg, presented a two-reel show dealing with mining, refining and transporting Chilean natural nitrate of soda. The program also showed twenty-four hours of growth of tobacco, tomato, and cotton plants "in three and a half seconds." The program was described as being, "of vital importance to all farmers."

The "Clemson College Motion Picture Truck" was in Orangeburg in March 1937. The newspaper article stated "Miss Louise C. Fleming, Home Agent, or Miss Matilda Bell, Assistant Home Agent, will accompany the truck. The pictures were shown under the auspices of the Home Demonstration Clubs.

Star Theatre
29 N Broughton Ave

An advertisement in *The Times and Democrat* newspaper dated December 7, 1912, states, "You will go wild with patriotic enthusiasm when you see "When Uncle Sam Was Young." The film showing was a two-reel 101 Bison Feature that included scenes of the Declaration of Independence, the Boston Tea Party, and Bunker Hill. Shows ran from 3 pm until 10:45 pm.

Bluebird Theatre
49 E Russell Street

The Bluebird Theater opened in September 1916. An advertisement at the time described a combination of plays and motion pictures. For twenty-five cents, you saw both the play and the movie. Programs changed daily.

The *Cahn and Hill Theatrical Guide and Moving Picture Directory* of 1921 lists the Bluebird Theater with 225 seats, and states that Mr. J. Harold Ziegler was the manager. The Bluebird Theatre was designated as a moving picture theater. In 1929, the Bluebird Theatre was offering feature movies for as little as ten cents. Their advertisements claimed "Big Pictures at Little Prices."

Reliance Theatre
44 W Russell Street

An early Orangeburg theater that provided both live stage shows and motion pictures, the Reliance Theater operated from about 1914 to about 1940.

The *Cahn and Hill Theatrical Guide and Moving Picture Directory* of 1921 lists the Reliance Theater as a 350 seat house providing Vaudeville and motion pictures under the management of Mr. J. Harold Zeigler.

Edisto Theatre
42 W Russell Street

In 1941, a brand new movie theater, the Edisto, was opened next door to the closed Reliance. The Edisto was operated by the Sims family until it was leased in the 1960s to another company. It was closed in the 1980s with the building used only for storage until late 1996. The 1945 edition of *Film Daily Yearbook* lists the Edisto Theatre and indicates that it had 500 seats.

Carolina Theatre
222 S Middleton St.

The Carolina Theatre opened around 1927. It was grand and elegant with seating for 1000. The auditorium ceiling was 40 feet above. The ceiling of the stage area had a height of 70 feet. There were six dressing rooms near the stage. The proscenium arch was edged with handsome medallion carvings. Great gilded eagles with spread wings hung high on the walls. The plush seats were the best to be had and the box seating was luxurious. Near the projection room was a fine lounge. Ushers helped you to your seat and patrolled the auditorium to ensure good behavior.

Live shows came regularly to the Carolina Theatre. In the early 1930s, Bob Jennings, II, began running motion pictures. Some time later Max Bryant took over. In 1939, the Orangeburg Theater Company took over operation and Ray Linn became the manager.

In an article that appeared in *The Times and Democrat* shortly after the Carolina Theatre closed in 1969, Ray Linn discussed the many great, and near great stars who performed there, the music of three decades, and more movies than he could recall.

The biggest drawing card and publicity gimmick he remembered was the old Carolina Jackpot every Friday night. He said, "Everybody had to buy a ticket whether they went to the movie or not, and if their name was called they could still win the jackpot. It ran from $125 to $1000 and a lot of people won!"

Like many other large theaters, the Carolina Theater lost patrons when television came on the scene. The declining tickets sales meant less money to maintain such a large theater. When it finally closed, in December, 1969, the paint was chipped, the curtains in tatters, and the walls covered with graffiti. The newspaper proclaimed, "Old Lady Bows Out."

Advertisement for "The Stowaway" showing at the Carolina Theater

Blulebird Theatre (New)
44 W Russell Street

The current Bluebird Theatre is located on the site of the former Edisto Theatre. James H. Gressette, Jr., owner of the theater building, was aware of the search for a permanent home for the Orangeburg Part-Time Players, the local theater group of which he is a member. In December, 1996, he made the donation of the building to the OPTP. Since then, it has undergone extensive renovation and restoration. The name Bluebird was chosen at Gressette's request in honor of his grandfather, James Izlar Sims, one of the owners of the original Bluebird.

Palmetto Theatre

The *Cahn and Hill Theatrical Guide and Moving Picture Directory* of 1921 lists the Palmetto Theatre with 200 seats and Mr. Brown as manager. The Palmetto Theatre is not listed in the 1945 edition of *Film Daily Yearbook*.

Blulebird Theatre - Home of the Orangeburg Part-Time Players

PICKENS

Thanks to Mr. Robert D. McJunkin, the grandson of the woman who built the movie theater in Pickens, we now know more of its history. We also know that the Jefferson and Pic were the same theater and that the first theater, a wooden sturcture, was replaced by a more substantial stone structure. Below is the story he told us.

———————— ❧ ————————

I wanted to share some history with you. The Pic Theatre in Pickens was built by my grandmother, Myrtie H. Stevenson. I don't know the exact date, but it would have been in the 1930s because my mother used to sell tickets there and my father would come to the window to court her while she was on duty. They were married in 1938.

My grandmother named it the Jefferson Theatre in honor of her father, Jefferson Davis Holder. She hired someone to manage it for her. Originally it was built of wood. It was very controversial in that a fundamentalist minister constantly ranted and raved about how evil it was to have a liquor store on one end of Main Street and a movie theatre on the other. The church prayed for it to burn down, and it did. That is why my family became Presbyterians.

My grandmother was not easily deterred, so she rebuilt the theatre out of stone, where it stood (I like to think, proudly, as a monument against narrow-mindedness) for many years at the end of Main Street, even after it was closed. I note the picture you have, which shows that the years of being empty were not kind to it. The door on the right next to the ticket window was the entrance for whites, and the door on the left was the exit for whites. The door on the far right was the colored entrance and provided access to the balcony. I remember that when I was about six years old, my grandmother wanted me to see a certain picture and wanted my nanny to take me. She called the manager, who said that my nanny was not permitted to sit downstairs with the white people, but I could sit with her in the balcony. My grandmother sold it shortly before she died in 1948, and the new owners changed the name to Pic.

I enjoyed going to the movies with my friends. If you were under 12 years of age, the ticket was 9 cents. Popcorn was 10 cents. We would get a dime from our parents and pool the change to buy a box of popcorn that we would share.

Robert D. McJunkin
July 30, 2010

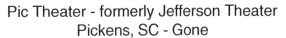

Pic Theater - formerly Jefferson Theater
Pickens, SC - Gone

Photograph courtesy of Wilton Porter

Rock Hill

Theatres of Rock Hill SC.
by Robert W. Ratterree Sr.
December 4, 2009

The Cinema Theatre on Oakland Ave in Rock Hill was right near Winthrop University. When it was new, I remember going to see the first "Star Wars" movie that came out. That will give you the starting date. It was sold to the Church because all the theatres were moving to the Malls and becoming multi-grouped theatres in one building. The single theatres couldn't compete anymore.

The Stevenson Theatre on Main Street up town was one of the best. When I was a kid I went to the Stevenson up until I graduated from high school. It was a good theatre to take your date too. Mom would give us fifty cents and send us to the theatre. Movies cost twenty-five cents to get in and we could get a coke and popcorn and have a nickel left over. I saw the first movie that scared me back then. It was called "The Blob." That night I dreamed that the Blob was coming through the heating vents to get me. Also saw the movie "Them," about giant ants. Dreamed about ants too.

The Capitol Theatre was the oldest in town that I remember. It closed about 1950. I remember going to it one time. Saw the movie "Amazon Women." Everything back then was B&W and was very close to being a non-talking movie. This theatre was a large room with a screen at the south end. Kind of like a sheet hung on the wall. The chairs were straight back oak chairs. No padded seats. Can you see some 7 year old kids sitting in oak chairs for 2 hours trying to watch a movie? That was the worst theatre I have ever been in. It cost a dime to get in. No drinks, no popcorn. I don't remember ever going back. I couldn't take those chairs again.

Carolina Theater - 1950
Tradd Main St.

The Carolina Theatre on Trade Street in Rock Hill was as good as the Stevenson. Good movies. The building was one of the original buildings on Trade. What I remember the most about the Carolina was your feet would stick to the floor from all the drinks spilled there. They must have never cleaned the floors in there at all. When you come in and go out, your feet would pop each time from breaking traction with the floor. The theatre itself was kind of dirty. Old dirty seats but the movies were good. This was in the early 1950s. Trade Street was built around 1886.

The Pix Theatre was one of the grandest theatres in South Carolina at the time. The Pix was owned by Bob Bryant and built in 1940. This ultra-modern, fireproof, air-conditioned theatre was one of the finest. It was designed by a team of architects from New York and was built for the cost of $100,000. I grew up going to this theatre. It was about a ½ mile from our home and we could walk to the theatre with no problem. I remember when the cost was fifteen cents and they raised the price up to twenty-five cents. Everybody in town wanted to boycott the theatre. But they kept coming. Then the price went to fifty cents and the whole town was up-in arms. No movie was worth fifty cents! This was the best theatre to take your dates too. Clean, nice and I can close my eyes and smell the popcorn and candy right now.

Stevenson Theater - 1955

Capitol Theater - 1955
Next to the Robert Marshall Hotel

Stevenson Theater - 1945
109 East Main St.

PIX Theater - Rock Hill - 1944

PIX Theater Auditorium - 1940

PIX Theater Projection Room - 1944

Dumb Waiter for Film Delivery

SALLEY

Memories of Salley
Joe L. Jones

Some will remember the blacksmith shop run by Mr. Boyd Yon, and the Livery Stable run by Mr. D. H. Salley. The Hotel was once popular with the traveling salesmen, who would arrive by train and stay over night. Even Coca-Cola was once bottled locally, and these old bottles, with the town's name, are collector's items.

In spite of its comparatively small size, Salley was one of the first towns outside of Columbia and Augusta to have its own theater in the 1930s, operated by H.A. Sawyer.

I lived next door to the Sawyers. I guess it was because H.A. knew me well that he asked me to run the projector. In fact, he probably knew I would be interested because I had one of those small projectors that families had.

I remember when we showed the movie "The Outlaw." Mr. Sawyer told me that we had a crowd coming from Columbia because they couldn't see it there.

(Note: One possible reason "The Outlaws" wasn't shown in Columbia was that it was, as Leonard Maltin describes it, "a Sex Western, introducing Jane Russell.")

I can say that we had a lot of "cowboys and Indians" movies. It was right popular for the teenagers. I don't know if they came as couples or just managed to end-up as couples in the seats after they got there.

I enjoyed operating the carbon-light projector, but not the patching of a film-strip. Since that time, I have wondered why I didn't cut a frame to save, especially from "The Outlaw", but it was probably new enough that it didn't break for me to patch.

My communication from the ticket office to the projector room was a water hose - it worked real good so I could be told when there were enough in the theatre for me to start the movie.

Salley boasted its own movie star in the late 1930s, 40s and 50s. She was Madelyn Earle Jones, a Salley native, who appeared in movies, on the stage and in radio as Lois Collier.

Sawyer Theater - Salley, SC

Lois Collier, one of Universal Studio's beautiful and talented actresses.

SALUDA

Saluda Theatre
107 Law Range
Opened 1936
National Register of Historic Places: 1993

Designed by Charles B. Thompson, the Saluda Theatre is a two-story, stuccoed masonry building in the Art Deco style.

The theatre and the building next to it were purchased in 1987 by members of the Saluda County Council. The Saluda County Historical Society began a process of restoring the theatre for community use and turning the adjacent building into a local history museum. The Saluda Theatre is currently home to the Saluda Players.

Jody Smith, an architect in Charleston, remembers going to the Saluda Theatre as a young boy. "Mr. Herlong was the manager. One Saturday, he yanked me out of my seat and sent me home for using a pea shooter during the movie."

Movie Actors Born in South Carolina

Frances Fuller (1907–1980) Charleston
Chief Bey (1913–2004) Yamassee
Deanie Gordon (1915–2010) Greenwood
Dizzy Gillespie (1917–1993) Cheraw
Mary Elliott (1917–2000) Gaffney
Lois Collier (1919–1999) Salley
Ann Savage (1921–2008) Columbia
Abigail Adams (1922–1955) Greenville
Stanley Donen (1924) Columbia
Alan Hood (1924) Marion
Virginia Capers (1925–2004) Sumter
Elizabeth Threatt (1926–1993) Kershaw
Eartha Kitt (1927–2008) North
Althea Gibson (1927–2003) Silver
Gloria Saunders (1927–1980) Columbia
Brook Benton (1931–1988) Camden
James Brown (1933–2006) Barnwell
Clarence Felder (1938) St. Matthews
Cale Yarborough (1939) Timmonsville
Bo Hopkins (1942) Greenville
Anthony James (1942) Myrtle Beach
Lauren Hutton (1943) Charleston
Larry Marshall (1944) Spartanburg
Alphonse Mouzon (1948) Charleston
Celia Weston (1951) Spartanburg
Alex English (1954) Columbia
Will Patton (1954) Charleston
Leeza Gibbons (1957) Hartsville
Thomas Gibson (1962) Charleston
Chris Rock (1965) Andrews
Viola Davis (1965) St. Matthews
Andy Dick (1965) Charleston
Melissa Wyler (1970) Myrtle Beach
Shawnee Smith (1970) Orangeburg

SPARTANBURG

We offer a sketch of the movie theaters of Spartanburg, aware that the theaters of Spartanburg have been covered in much richer and greater detail by Marion Peter Holt in his excellent book, "Magical Places, The Story of Spartanburg's Theatres and Their Entertainments:1900-1950" published by Hub City Writers Project in 2004.

Spartanburg had its share of arcades, nickelodeons, and store front movie houses. These included the Fairyland, Magic and Electric Theaters. These were soon followed by the Royal Palace and the Royal. Both of the "Royals" were combination houses, offering vaudeville and motion pictures.

The Lyric opened in 1909, on East Main Street. The location must have been good because, even though the name changed over the years, it was in operation until 1940. During those years it was known as the Tivoli, Majestic, Rialto, Omar, and, finally, the Criterion.

In 1910, the Grand Theater opened across the street from the Lyric, operated by Spartanburg's most interesting theater operator, Lawrence Lester, Jr. In 1913, Lester opened another theater on East Main Street and named it the Lester. In 1915, Lester sold both of his theaters. The Grand was renamed the Bijou and the beautiful 800-seat Lester Theater became the Strand.

The Rex opened in 1917. Also on East Main, the Rex boasted 1,000 seats. In 1918 the owners added a Moller theater organ to better compete with the Strand Theater. In his book, Marion Peter Holt explains that the people of Spartanburg didn't say "I'm going to the movies." Rather, they specified, "I'm going to the Rex" or "I'm going to the Strand." According to Holt, the Rialto didn't attract the ladies who disapproved of its live vaudeville acts they called "girlie shows."

In 1934 the Rialto, formerly the Lyric, was rewired for sound and became the Criterion Theater. Promoted by the management as "Spartanburg's Family Theater" the Criterion closed in 1940 and the space became a retail shop. The building was demolished in the late 1980s.

1936 advertisement for the Strand Theater promoting 15 cents admission for all seats all hours

Rex Theater - March 12, 1920

Rex Theater - Spartanburg
from Marion Peter Holt

Photo courtesy of Marion Peter Holt

In 1934, the Rex, which had closed in 1929, installed sound equipment and opened as the State. A live stage show, "Ten Minute Break," an all-soldier musical revue co-authored by David Reid, was performed by the enlisted men at Camp Croft at the State Theatre in 1943. In 1967 the State became the Capri, but a fire damaged the theater's roof and auditorium and it closed. The owners gutted the interior rather than invest in its costly repairs.

Photograph provided by
South Carolina Department of Archives and History.

The Palmetto Theatre, a first-run theater designed by Erle G. Stillwell, was built in 1940. It had the most up-to-date projection and sound systems. It had staggered seating so no person's view was blocked by the person seated in front of them. In addition to the main floor, the Palmetto had double balconies.

In the 1950s, the Palmetto was unable to make the transition to Cinemascope effectively. It did host a number of popular 3-D movies of the era. It faded away showing X-rated films and closed in 1972.

The Palmetto Theater was added to the National Register of Historic Places in 1996. Closed since the mid-1970s, the roof of the theater collapsed in 1980 and, in 2003, the building was demolished.

The only single-screen movie theater still standing in Spartanburg is the Carolina. Built in 1925 and originally called Montgomery Theater, it is in the Montgomery Building on the corner of North Church and St. John Streets. In the early days, there were more live theater events presented than motion pictures. The Montgomery Theater showed "The Jazz Singer" in 1928 to sold out performances for a week.

It became the Carolina when the Wilby-Kinsey chain took over operation in 1932. An advertisement for the movie "San Francisco" playing at the Carolina in 1936, sported a snow covered Carolina Theater logo and a tag line saying, "Last week during the terrific hot spell your Carolina was a haven of comfort for thousands. You too can escape the heat… see a good show… in cool comfort for only 25 cents until 6 pm – 30 cents after 6."

The theater was given a thrifty and dismal renovation in 1970, losing many of its desirable decorative elements. The Carolina closed in 1978. It is hoped this beautiful theater will be restored and once again serve the community in Spartanburg.

Carolina Theater - Spartanburg

ST. GEORGE

A 1923 Sanborn Map shows a "Movie" theater at 222 N. Main street. This theater had a balcony. No other information was available.

Lourie Theatre in 2003

The Lourie Theatre was built in 1929. In an article in Charleston's *The Post and Courier* dated August 20, 1997, Mr. Holcomb Blume recalls running the projector at the Lourie Theatre for twenty-five years. He said, "Channel 5 television opened up in Charleston, and that killed the Lourie Theatre."

But, the Lourie Theatre is doing well. A $20,000 state Parks, Recreation and Tourism grant awarded through the Heritage Corridor Foundation in 2000, was designated for building a larger stage, orchestra pit, dressing rooms, restrooms and adding more seats. This allowed the old silent movie house to put on full stage productions.

The theatre was nearly lost to a major fire in September, 2005. The fire destroyed three century-old buildings before 100 firefighters from four counties brought it under control. The Lourie Theater was spared.

ST. MATTHEWS

In the September 16, 1936 issue of the *Times and Democrat*, we learn that St. Matthews will get a new movie theater.

> The lot on West Railroad Avenue is being cleared for the erection of an up-to-date moving picture house, the cost of which will be more than $5,000. The lot belonged to the South Carolina National Bank here and was bought by J.W. Wactor and T.M. Ulmer of Holly Hill, who will erect the building at once. The building and equipment will be up-to-date in every respect.

In 2006, Dr. Robert E. Homan recalled the St. Matthews movie theater in his column "Precious Memories" in the *Times and Democrat*.

> In 1935 Marley Ulmer from Holly Hill opened the Calhoun Theater on West Bridge Street, between Prof. Ford's Barber Shop and Berger's Shoe Shop, across from the offices of the J.L. Carroll Livery Stable. Johnny Murray, also from Holly Hill, and his beautiful little blond wife moved to St. Matthews to operate the cinema. Johnny was the projectionist. Mrs. Murray sold tickets.

> Gilbert (Gilly) Smoak took up tickets and did the maintenance. Gilly was assisted with the cleaning chores by a host of little boys he picked up off the street. He would speak to them in "Tarzanese," which he learned from watching too many Tarzan movies.

SULLIVAN'S ISLAND

Post Theater - 1454 Middle Street

Suzannah Smith Miles on the Post Theater

I recall well the movie house on Sullivan's Island. It was originally the Post Theater for Fort Moultrie and, in my lifetime, active in the fifties and early sixties as the Island Theater. You purchased the ticket from the window outside. Once in, you entered a concession area. Two entrances from either side led into the theater, which was small. I think there was a balcony.

I was seated in the balcony when, scared out of my wits, I screamed out loud to a scene from "House on Haunted Hill." Maybe it was "Pit and the Pendulum." I remember seeing both there, as well as a very guilty viewing of "Peyton Place" which I had been expressly forbidden to see. The girl's bathroom, which had a window to the outside, provided a most suitable entrance if one did not have enough money to buy a ticket. I don't think they were open every night, probably only on weekends, and I'm not sure they were open during the wintertime. Sullivan's Island back then pretty much closed up in the winter.

SUMMERVILLE

The James F. Dean Community Theatre, at 133 South Main Street, opened as a movie theater in 1935. It was know locally as "The Show." It was a successful movie theater from its opening until the mid-1960's.

"The Show" in 1940

The Flowertown Players, a community theater group, was founded in 1976. They bought the 209-seat theater and named it the James F. Dean Community Theatre for one of its founders. The theater is listed as part of the Historic District in the National Register of Historic Places.

James F. Dean Community Theatre

SUMTER

Sumter Opera House

The Opera House was built around 1893. In 1936 the Opera House was renovated into a movie theater. The first film shown at the Opera House was "Earthworm Tractors." Tickets in those days were 35 cents for adults and 10 cents for children.

During its tenure as a movie theater the Opera House underwent several changes. In 1973 it was officially listed on the National Register of Historical Places. In 1982 the Opera House closed its doors after 46 years of operation as a movie theater.

Sumter Opera House as Sumter Theater
in the mid-1970s

The City of Sumter purchased the building in 1984 and began a restoration of the Opera House. The Opera House still houses City Hall and many of the City's departments and offices, including City Council's chambers. The first floor auditorium is popular, and hosts local, regional, and national talent on a regular basis.

"Moving Picture World" Volume 3 (1908)

Sumter, SC – Of the three moving picture theaters here the Lyric is the best appointed and the S.R.O. sign is frequently seen. The Elite is another finely equipped house and caters to the best society in town. The Gem, for colored patrons, is an extension of the Elite, divided only by the screen, the same pictures serving for both houses. The Gem has its entrance on a back street and the only additional expense is the ticket seller and ticket taker. Although the same program is seen in both places, the admission to the Gem is five cents, while ten cents admits to the more finely appointed Elite.

Movie-going was an important source of entertainment during the 1920s and 1930s, and every town of any size in South Carolina had a movie theater in the downtown shopping district. The Rex Theater in Sumter held special showings for school children, and promoted the movies they booked with flyers promising a free cookie and soft drink.

The 1912 Sanborn Map of Sumter shows a "Motion Picture Tent" on the corner of South Main and Caldwell Streets. It was located next to a "Shooting Gallery."

In the 1920 edition of the *Cahn and Hill Directory of Motion Picture Theaters*, the Academy of Music is listed with 900 seats, the Lyric Theater with 300 seats, and the Rex with 400 seats.

The 1927 *Film Year Book* lists the Garden Theater (Colored) with 200 seats, the Rex with 400 seats and the Victory Theater with 200 seats. There is no realistic expectation of finding all of the movie theaters in Sumter, nor of identifying there locations.

In an article by Mayor "Bubba" McElveen in *The Item* dated December 17, 2005, the Roxy Theater is mentioned. It was on Manning Avenue and open for less than a year. The location became a washerette.

The 1945 edition of *Film Daily Yearbook* lists the Carolina Theater with 800 seats, the Lyric with 300 seats, the Rex with 500 seats and the Sumter with 800 seats.

This photo is identified as the Rex Theater on Liberty Street. The 1915 Sanborn Map of Sumter clearly shows the Rex Theater at 10-12 North Main Street. This may have been another Rex Theater.

Lyric Theater
Photos courtesy of Mayor "Bubba" McElveen

WALTERBORO

Cindy and John Corley operate the Old Bank Christmas and Gifts shop in Walterboro. Cindy remembered the Cook Theater and smiled broadly as she told us her memories.

"When I was a child this was a very busy street. All the stores were full. Everybody knew everybody. My mother worked at Infinger's. If I was good all week long and swept the floors and emptied the ash trays, back then people could smoke in the stores, kept the bathrooms clean, then, on Saturday they would give me a dollar.

I would walk down the street to the Cook Theater and watch the Saturday matinee. For that dollar, I could get my ticket, popcorn, coke, and two different kinds of candy.

My father was the jeweler here. I would sit in the theater and watch the advertising before the movie. Across the screen in blue and silver it would say, "Infinger's Jewelers. If you don't know jewelry, know your jeweler." That was my father's motto, and I used to be so proud to see our name up on that big movie screen.

Mr. Henry Cook also knew my mother and if I talked in the movie, he would call my mother and tell her I talked and then for two Saturdays I couldn't go to the movies."

Ritz Theater 1937-1956
Drawing by Bob Grenko of Walterboro

Walterboro's Theaters
by Mr. Henry Belk Cook
August 11, 2004

My father opened the Ritz Theater in 1937 or 1938. The old theater was around the corner on Railroad Avenue. It burned down. It was called the New Era Theater. My father opened a theater down the street next to the grocery store.

My father leased what used to be the Chevrolet dealership here (329 Washington Street) from Mr. Chapel. He had to make the building taller. They built the roof the best they could back in those days. Every time it rained, the roof would leak. Mr. Chapel got tired of fixing the roof and he asked my daddy, "Do you want to buy this old building?" He said, "Yeah, how much you want for it?" He told him and my daddy bought it.

"Gone With The Wind" opened here at the Ritz Theater in 1939. Everybody wanted to see "Gone With The Wind." I remember we had to number the seats so we could sell tickets for reserved seats. We put tape on every seat. We numbered the rows, "A, B, and C" and the seats, "1, 2, 3" and sold tickets from a grid on a piece of paper.

The Ritz had a big balcony. Blacks entered through a separate door. The woman in the ticket booth just made a quarter-turn and sold tickets through another window to the black patrons. The balcony had the best seats in the house.

In the auditorium, the seats ran down almost to the edge of the stage. The stage was about five feet deep. The screen hung in there. It was almost square in shape, not wide like today.

We had a big "squirrel cage" blower with a ten horse motor to keep the place cool. It had four speeds on it. It circulated water that ran down into a catch basin. The fan blew a mist. It worked real good.

We had a deep lobby with a terrazzo floor. The projectors were upstairs. The box office was at the back of the lobby. We sold popcorn in the front. There were candy machines in the lobby. There were two stores, one on either side of the lobby. There was a soda fountain on one side. There was a beauty shop on the other side.

Hot dogs were a nickel and hamburgers were a dime. Coca-Cola was six cents. You could get ice cream in the soda shop for a nickel a dip."

We built the Cook Theater, around the corner in 1948. After the Cook Theater opened, we kept the Ritz Theater open mostly on weekends and showed Westerns.

Cook Theater 1947-1986
Drawing by Bob Grenko of Walterboro

VARNVILLE

William Harrell Rentz
February 8, 1891 - August 10, 1933
Varnville, South Carolina

Vaco Theatre - 1915

William Harrell Rentz opened the VACO Theatre, the first movie theater in Varnville, South Carolina, in 1915. In 1917, a fire destroyed a section of downtown Varnville, including the movie theater. Mr. Rentz provided continued film screenings in an outdoor setting until he could open another theater.

He opened the Strand Theatre in 1919. A Clemson graduate with a degree in Civil Engineering, Mr. Rentz was a friend and mentor to Gerald Meeks, who took over theater operations in 1924. The 1921 edition of *The Julius Cahn - Gus Hill Theatrical Guide and Moving Picture Directory* states that Mr. Rentz also managed the Pastime Theatre in Allendale, South Carolina.

Strand Theatre building

William Harrell Rentz playing cards with himself.
Trick photograph taken around 1920.

Strand Theater advertisement
in the *Hampton County Guardian*
May 9, 1934

STRAND
THEATRE
VARNVILLE, S. C.

Friday and Saturday
May 11 and 12
'AFTER TONIGHT'

May 18 and 19

May 15 and 16
'CHANCE AT HEAVEN'

Friday and Saturday
Tuesday and Wednesday
'MORNING GLORY'

First Show 7:45
Second Show 9:00
Adm. 11c & 25c

YORK

Above: Sylvia Theater in 2009. Left: Sylvia Theater around 1950.

Sylvia Theater

The Sylvia Theater was formerly the Shandon Hotel, built in 1904. In the 1930s, a York resident purchased the hotel and removed the second floor. He created a balcony and a projection room. He named the theater after his daughter. The theater closed in the late 1960s and at various times was a teacher supply shop and hardware store. The building is on the National Register of Historic Places.

Paul Finnican came to York to close on a business loan deal sometime in the summer of 2001. He saw this "diamond in the rough" building in the revitalized downtown area of York, immediately fell in love and started asking questions. Paul saw the unrealized potential and architectural integrity of the 100 year old building, coupled that with his desire to provide a venue for the singer-songwriter in this particular area and proceeded to purchase and personally renovate it.

After completely redoing the interior and adding some nice touches, like re-sawing some of the beautiful, 100 year old beams to make the stage floor and bar top, The Sylvia Theater has been brought back to her well deserved status as a place to enjoy the arts. The true nature of this venue has been brought to fruition by the tireless work of Paul, his family and friends, and by the well wishing and earnest folks of the York community.

AFRICAN AMERICAN THEATERS

The history of single-screen movie theaters in South Carolina cannot be told without mentioning racial segregation. Local and state laws specifically prohibited white and African-American citizens from sharing transportation, accommodations, schools, restaurants, public restrooms and water fountains. It was the law. Until the United States Supreme Court ruled in the *Brown v Board of Education* case in 1954, the policy in the southern states was segregation of the races. Even then, racial segregation in movie theaters remained a fact of life into the 1970s.

The most common method of enforcing segregation was to restrict the whites to the auditorium or ground floor, while restricting African-Americans to the balcony of the theater. This was so strictly enforced that blacks and whites had separate ticket windows and separate entrances. When a theater had no balcony, other arrangements were made. In the case of the O'Berry Theater in Ellenton, South Carolina, a wooden railing was constructed down the middle of the theater. African-Americans sat on the left side and whites sat on the right side.

Some towns made no accommodation for African-Americans and advertised their theaters as "For Whites Only." Many communities had separate theaters for the races. Some of the African-American movie theaters were operated by whites and some were owned and operated by African-Americans.

African American theaters came into existence in the 1890s. In an African American theater, one could enter through the front door without fear and occupy the best seat in the house. Like all theaters of the period, live entertainment was mixed with motion pictures.

These theaters gave rise to companies of performers and several motion picture companies that produced entertainment for African American audiences. These productions showed African Americans in the full range of social life and were not limited to the stereotypes portrayed on stage and in films produced by white companies.

Oscar Michauex, a pioneer African-American film director, made movies with "An All Colored Cast." His film "Underworld" was shown at the Harlem Theater in Laurens, in 1948.

Poster for Michauex's "Underworld."

The Harlem Theater, in Laurens, S.C., was operated for African American audiences during segregation. Mr. R.L. Higgins was listed as manager in the advertisement in 1948.

HARLEM THEATRE

Sunday Night Late Show—12:05
—OCT. 17—
HUNTED! TO THE ENDS OF THE EARTH!
Escape Impossible — — —
"UNDERWORLD"
—with—
AN ALL-COLORED—ALL-STAR CAST

MON., OCT. 18   TUES., OCT. 19
"RHAPSODY IN BLUE"
—featuring—
THE QUEEN OF THE KEYBOARD
"Hazel Scott"
ROBERT ALDA———————JOAN LESLIE
COMEDY————————ALL AMERICAN NEWS
Monday Morning Show at 10

WED., OCT. 20   THURS., OCT. 21
HE BELONGS TO ME FOR KEEPS!
"THAT MAN OF MINE"
—with—
AN ALL-COLORED—ALL-STAR CAST
PATHE NEWS————CHAPT. No. 14 "JUNGLE GIRL"
Wednesday Morning Show at 10

FRI., OCT. 22   SAT., OCT. 23
BOB STEELE in
"BILLY THE KID OUTLAWED"
—also—
ALAN LADD in
"BLACK CAT"
——LOOK THEM OVER——
Saturday Morning Show at 10

I know all pictures on this program will please you.—R. L. Higgins, Mgr.

Laurens Advertiser - October 14, 1948

While most of the films shown at the Harlem Theater were intended for African-American audiences, there was still the traditional Western movie shown on Saturday

In Charleston, the Lincoln Theater, located on King Street, offered live shows and movies to the African-American community from the early 1920s until 1972.

The theater was run by Damon Ireland Thomas, who was a regular columnist for the *Chicago Defender* and a close personal friend of Oscar Michauex.

One patron we interviewed had fond memories of the Lincoln Theater. Sharon Drayton, of Charleston, recalled going to the Lincoln Theater as a young girl.

"My elementary school gave out free tickets. My mom would give me a dollar. At that time you thought you were rich, you know. I had twenty-five cents for a box of popcorn and twenty-five cents for a soda. The first movie I saw there was "Cotton Comes to Harlem."

A group of girls would meet up with a group of boys and we'd go to the Lincoln Theater. On a Saturday, when you'd done your chores you got to go to the movies. It was just fun.

As we got older and it was going to close down, we tried to get a petition to save it. But, the manager said the theater was old and the cost of repairs to fix it wasn't worth it.

We loved that movie theater. When it was announced in the paper that it was going to close down, all who remembered it, all who attended it when they were young went to the matinee. That whole Saturday, from ten in the morning until about eight that evening, they had all the movies that were shown there. They showed all the movies to the end and then there was no more. So, that's when everybody started going down to the Riviera Theater."

The Lincoln Theater closed in 1972. The building was severely damaged by Hurricane Hugo in September, 1989, and was torn down on November 9, 1989.

Another Lincoln Theater we encountered was located in Bennettsville, South Carolina.

Lincoln Theater building - photo 2008

The Lincoln Theatre was located at the corner of Liberty and Market Streets in Bennettsville, in an area known as the Gulf. Carolina B. Breeden, a well known African American businessman, owned the theater. Mr. Breeden was born in Marlboro County in 1866. A business partner, Heber Covington, was the theater's general manager. During the 1940s and 1950s, Carl and Henry Crosland ran the theater. Their sister, Mamie Crosland Johnakin sold tickets. Luther Johnakin sold peanuts and candy.

In his book, "Rediscovering the Gulf: Bennettsville's Colored Business District, 1876 – 1976" Jerry T. Kendall interviewed Mark Covington. In the interview, Mr. Covington, who was born in Clio, S.C. in 1923, recalled that boxing matches were held at the theater. Blacks and Whites competed. Blacks and Whites also attended the matches. Whites sat in the balcony and Blacks sat on the ground floor.

The theater was always popular and contributed to the entertainment of local people as well as people from the surrounding farms. On a typical weekend in the 1920s and into the 1940s, the streets in the Gulf were crowded with as many as two hundred people. The theater closed sometime in the mid-1950s. Today, the building is occupied by Marlboro Engineering, Inc.

The Carver Theater, in Columbia, was located at 1519 Harden Street across from Benedict College. Below is a brief description of the Carver Theater by the South Carolina State Historic Preservation Office

The Carver Theatre was important to the community because it was one of only two theaters where African Americans were free to go to the movies. The theater was built about 1941 next to the Waverly community, the pre-eminent black neighborhood of professionals, physicians, nurses, educators, ministers, and skilled tradesmen. Not only were movies shown there, but the theater also had weekly talent shows, patterned after the famous "Amateur Hour" in Harlem, for young people in the area. Because of its history and importance to the neighborhood, Carver Theatre was listed in the National Register of Historic Places on July 17, 2003.

Interior of Carver Theater - Columbia

MOVIE THEATERS AND THE MILITARY IN SOUTH CAROLINA

SOUTH CAROLINA THEATERS DURING WORLD WAR I

When war erupted in Europe in 1914, the United States tried to remain neutral. People in South Carolina were still feeling the aftermath of the Civil War. There really wasn't much interest in South Carolina for what would become known as the Great War.

In 1915, the Lusitania was sunk without warning by a German submarine, killing 120 Americans. After more attacks on American merchant ships, President Wilson asked Congress to declare war on Germany, which it did on April 6, 1917.

Every newspaper in South Carolina carried reports of the war and encouraged local support. Local efforts to support our troops included food drives, rallies, parades, concerts and fund raising events. Speeches in support of the war were drawing large crowds in town squares, movie houses and other theaters.

Ship building was essential for the war effort and the Charleston Navy Shipyard expanded. Camp Jackson in Columbia grew to over 1,500 buildings, including theaters, stores, barracks, training facilities, stables, warehouses, and an airfield. As of December 31, 1917, there was a total military strength of 42,498 soldiers at Camp Jackson.

Trolley cars connected the camp with downtown, allowing soldiers to shop and participate in social activities such as dances and theater outings.

With American forces joining the Allies in Europe, Germany finally agreed to a cease-fire. On November 11, 1918, the Allies celebrated victory and the end of the Great War.

Theater at Camp Jackson in 1918

"The Price of Peace" shown at the Strand Theater in Varnville

During World War I, Hampton County held a "Victory Liberty Loan Campaign" similar to the "Buy War Bonds" efforts later used during World War II. An automobile tour of Hampton County was organized that included prominent speakers, singers and entertainers from Camp Jackson. At each scheduled stop, the people who gathered were entertained "in oratory and song" and appeals were made for money for the Victory Liberty Loan drive.

On Friday, May 9, 1919, the movie "The Price of Peace" was shown at both the matinee and evening shows at the Strand Theatre in Varnville. This movie was the "official picture which purports to cover our part in the Great War from the day it was declared to date." The movie, which was part of the Victory Liberty Loan Campaign, was shown free of charge.

The campaign ended on Sunday in Hampton with a demonstration of a military tank and a monster basket picnic on the courthouse square.

These "Victory Liberty Loan Campaign" events continued after Armistice Day in order to pay off the debt resulting from the war.

The deadly Spanish Flu outbreak occurred just as The Great War began to wind down. World-wide the Spanish influenza epidemic killed 20 million people. In South Carolina, there were an estimated 170,000 influenza cases and 6,100 deaths.

South Carolina experienced its first serious outbreak of influenza during the spring of 1918. This outbreak occurred at a military base, Camp Sevier, which was located near Greenville.

Hospitals in Columbia were overwhelmed by the epidemic. The hospital at Camp Jackson was expanded, allowing it to treat more than 5000 flu victims throughout the time of the crisis.

During the peak of the 1918 influenza pandemic, the US Navy operated hospitals in Charleston and at Parris Island.

Theaters, schools, churches and most other public places closed during the Spanish Enfluenza epidemic of 1918.

In October, 1918, it was announced by Pastime Amusement Company of Charleston that, "as soon as the Spanish influenza quarantine is lifted, the Victory Theatre (formerly the Victoria Theater) will be opened. In view of the glorious record of the U.S. in the war to crush the Prussian government, Mr. Sottile decided to re-christen the house, and it will henceforth be known as the Victory."

Aiken Journal
February 12, 1919

The influenza situation has improved to such an extent in Gaffney that the board of health has allowed the schools and theaters to open and there were services in all of the churches. There are still a number of cases, but they are on the decline, and it is hoped that it has run its course.

SOUTH CAROLINA THEATERS DURING WORLD WAR II

First Movies Shown on Sundays

Movies were not shown on Sundays in South Carolina until World War II. The laws were relaxed in order to provide entertainment to the large number of soldiers stationed in the state during the war. In addition to the existing Army and Navy facilities in South Caroilna at the time, a large military training center was built in 1941 near Spartanburg. Camp Croft hosted 75,000 soldiers a year from 1941 until it closed in 1946. It had four theaters. They were used for training films and lectures during the day and to show movies at night.

Camp Croft, South Carolina 1940-1947

Interview with Andrew J. Daley
June 18, 2006

When I was drafted in 1941, I was supposed to go in for one year compulsive military training and then be discharged. But, I was drafted in June and on December 7th, the Japanese bombed Pearl Harbor. I remember Franklin Roosevelt on the radio saying we were in for the duration of the war.

I took my basic training at Camp Croft (near Spartanburg, SC.) The camp was new, and they were looking for somebody to run the projectors in the theaters. Anytime you're inducted into the service, they want to know what you've done. If you're a flyer, they put you in the Air Force. They place you where they can use you best.

Note: All photographs of Camp Croft in this section courtesy of Jack Daley and Andrew J. Daley

Andrew J. Daley

They needed somebody who understood projectors for these four theaters. They weren't like these 16mm table projector models. They were these big things like they use in the Radio City Music Hall. They were Simplex projectors with Peerless lamps and RCA sound like I was running in civilian life. The Simplex was the advanced model, the latest thing.

Projection Room - Camp Croft

One of four theaters at Camp Croft near Spartanburg

When I went to Camp Croft we got paid $21 a month. They fed you, they gave you clothes, they gave you a bed to sleep and you became government property. You did what they told you. They would say, "When you were home, you did it your way. Now, you're here and you're going to do it our way."

After basic training, they put me in the projection booth. They gave me a Jeep and a Sergeant's rating. There were three white theaters and one black theater. Back in those days the colored people were by themselves. They trained by themselves and they even had their own theater.

We had drivers who shuttled the films between the theaters. There was this one colored driver who shuttled the film between theater 1 and theater 4. He would deliver the film and wait for it. So, he began to watch the fellows while they threaded up the film and showed it. It was my job to keep the picture on the screen and I needed somebody at the black theater so I told him, "You can do this." So, I had a colored projectionist too.

I was in the military four-and-a-half years. When I got out, I went back where I worked before the war. You know, the government said, "He got drafted. It wasn't his fault. So, when he gets back, you should give him his job back." But, somebody had my job.

Not long ago my son Jack and I flew down to Camp Croft. When we got there, we found out there was going to be a fifty-year celebration at the end of the month. So, we went back for that. I went over the roster of those who were there but I didn't see the name of anyone I knew. You know, when you get right down to it, most of the World War II vets aren't here anymore. For my age, I'm doing pretty good.

We would like to express our appreciation to Jack Daley for arranging an interview with his father and to Andrew J. Daley for sharing his memories of Camp Croft. We also appreciate the many photographs Mr. Daley shared from his collection.

Berry Grable at Camp Croft

A performer from Betty Grable show at typewriter in Camp Croft theater office with Andrew J. Daley

Berry Grable on stage at Camp Croft Theater

WAR DEPT. THEATERS

CAMP CROFT, S. C.

Program - One Week, Starting 11 Aug 1945

FOR POST DISTRIBUTION ONLY

ALL DOUBLE FEATURE PROGRAMS START AT 1800 AND 2000

THEATER NO 1 — 1800 - 2000 Sunday — 1330 - 1730 - 1930 THEATER NO. 3 — 1835 - 2035 Sunday — 1415 - 1805 - 2005	DATE	THEATER NO. 2 — 1835 - 2035 Sunday — 1415 - 1805 - 2005 THEATER NO. 4 — 1800 - 2000 Sunday — 1330 - 1730 - 1930
Double Feature Program **"THE WOMAN IN GREEN"** —and— **"MAMA LOVES PAPA"**	Saturday **11** **Aug**	Claudette Colbert Don Ameche —in— **"GUEST WIFE"** Dick Foran
Robert Cummings Lizabeth Scott —in— **"YOU CAME ALONG"** —also— The Latest News of the Day	Sunday **12** **Aug**	—also— Californy 'Er Bust The Latest News of the Day
	Monday **13** **Aug**	Double Feature Program **"THE WOMAN IN GREEN"** —and— **"MAMA LOVES PAPA"**
James Craig Signe Hasso —in— **"DANGEROUS PARTNERS"** This Is America Cartoon	Tuesday **14** **Aug**	Robert Cummings Lizabeth Scott —in— **"YOU CAME ALONG"**
James Stewart Paulette Goddard —in— **"JIMMY STEPS OUT"** (A Reissue) The Silver Streak Mexican Playland	Wednesday **15** **Aug**	 —also— The Latest News of the Day
George Raft Signe Hasso —in— **"JOHNNY ANGEL"**	Thursday **16** **Aug**	James Craig Signe Hasso —in— **"DANGEROUS PARTNERS"** This Is America Cartoon
—also— Army-Navy Screen Magazine The Latest News of the Day	Friday **17** **Aug**	James Stewart Paulette Goddard —in— **"JIMMY STEPS OUT"** (A Reissue) The Silver Streak Mexican Playland

Box Office Opens 15 Minutes Prior to Hours Given Above

BAND & WHITE, PRINTERS, SPARTANBURG, S. C.

"In 1947, the entire acreage of the former Camp Croft was declared surplus by the War Assets Administration. By 1950, the Army sold the land by pieces to organizations and businesses, including the transfer of 7,088 acres of land to the South Carolina Commission of Forestry for the creation of the Croft State Park. The remaining acreage has been converted to residential housing, and industrial and commercial businesses." - Ron Crawley, South Carolina History Net

War Bond Rally on steps of South Carolina State House

Columbia

After performing at Camp Croft in Spartanburg, Betty traveled to Columbia to promote War Bond sales at a rally on Main Street. A lock of her hair was offered as a prize to the largest bond purchase.

At right: Betty Grable having a lock of her hair cut

Note: All photographs of Columbia in this section from the collection of Malcolm Samuel Suggs, City Manager of the Columbia Theaters in the Wilby-Kincey Theater Chain.

Carolina Theater - Columbia - 1942

Strand Theater - Columbia - 1943

Ritz Theater - Columbia - 1942

5 Points Theater - Columbia - 1942

Women in uniform wait at Gloria Theater in Charleston to see "Salute to the Marines" - 1943

The Augusta Chronicle
December 10, 1941

Mrs. S.J. Wilson has announced that in line with National Defense Work and aid to Britain, a feature movie will be given Friday afternoon at the Carolina Theatre in Allendale, with admission free. Each patron is expected to bring a gift of warm clothing, which can be sent to the British wrapped in Christmas packages.

Former Carolina Theater
in Allendale

Former Chesterfield Theater
Now a flower shop

Chesterfield
Praying for Our Troops

During WWII, the fire station in Chesterfield would sound its siren three times at noon. Those who could gathered in the Chesterfield Theater and prayed for the safety of our soldiers overseas. It wasn't a formal event. People just went into the theater, sat down and prayed silently for a while. Then, they went on with their business.

THE MILL VILLAGE AND THE MOVIES

The cotton mills in South Carolina employed thousands of people during the 1920s to 1970s. Small housing developments were built for the mill workers. These mill villages were often served by a mill company store. Aiken County Stores served several of South Carolina's cotton mill towns. Anything a mill worker needed could be bought at the company store, including food, cloth, shoes, and fuel. One account we have read stated that even coffins were available at the company store.

The mill village was built so that a worker never had to leave. While the size and character of each mill village was different, they often included a drugstore, lunch counter, barber shop, bank, post office and jail. Some of the company stores had a large room above for meetings, box suppers, dances, and showing movies.

Workers in the cotton mills worked long hours and were paid little. The work was hard, dirty, and dangerous. The mill offered a self-perpetuating culture and a closed economy. Many workers were paid in scrip. This could be spent like cash in the businesses in the mill village. Sometimes, the towns nearby would accept scrip in payment. If a worker ran low on cash, he could go to the mill office and get an advance in the form of tokens called "loonies" or "dugaloos." He could spend them at the store and have the amount deducted from his pay.

Gerald Bratcher, of Honea Path, told us that mill workers often came to his father's barber shop in Anderson. He told us, "There are three kinds of haircuts. For cash you'd get a good haircut. For credit you'd get a fair haircut. For mill tokens you'd hardly get a haircut at all."

Many of the mills operated on shifts. Movies were sometimes scheduled in the mornings to accommodate those on night shifts. The importance of the motion pictures to residents of these mill villages is apparent in an interview done as part of a Works Progress Administration (WPA) oral history project in August, 1938. The interviewer asked the wife of a mill worker to describe a typical day in her life.

"You'd like to know what a day in my life is like? Well, taint no trouble at all for me to tell you because every one is so much like the other I've learned the pattern by heart long ago.

The year goes round bringin' very little change but the weather. Poor folks don't have no vacation, you know, when they's time off from cooking, and washing, and worrying about the grocery bill. The only money I've spent for pleasure this year went for the picture show and for them flowers. I'm glad my flowers done so well. Hit's nicer settin' on the porch when they's somethin' to look at besides a red, ugly hill.

Next day starts like the one before and ends about the same. Of course, on Fridays and Saturdays hits a little different. Both of us enjoys Westerns and we gen'ly go once a week to the picture show. I go on Friday night while he stays with the children and then he goes on Saturday. They's always a bunch of women goin' on Friday and I go along with them. Hit'd be nice if me and him could go together sometimes but they's nobody to leave the children with.

If it wasn't for that movie I don't know what I'd do. Course, we ain't really able to spend the 15¢ apiece for foolishness when he's just makin' nine dollars and sixty cent a week, but a body cain't stand it if he don't have a little pleasure sometimes."

The woman describes a dreary situation and it is important to keep some historical perspective on life in a mill village. These mill towns grew up at a time when much of the south was moving from a farm economy to one that included industrial development. For many who worked in the cotton mills and lumber mills, this meant a regular paycheck, access to medical care, and a social life that was not available on the family farm. The mill villages of South Carolina existed in a unique period of history. That culture is fading from memory.

ALCOLU, SC

Alcolu was established between 1885 and 1890 as a mill town for the Alderman Lumber Company. Like many of the theatres in the mill villages of South Carolina, the Alcolu Theatre was a large auditorium built above the company store. The only entrance to the theatre is by way of steep metal stairs at the back of the store. Movies were shown but the space was also used for meetings, dances, and live shows.

The small village of Alcolu is all but gone. The company store sits on a small section of road, now bypassed by newer highway construction on Route 521 in Clarendon County. It is between Manning and Sumter but not close enough to be included in the activities of either city.

As a company town, everyone worked at the mill, took scrip to the company store, and could buy groceries, see the doctor, or watch a show in the 200 seat theater upstairs. The Alcolu Sawmill and Burkes Brothers Store remains today as a living testament to the town origins.

Alcolu, SC - Mill Village store with theater in 1938. Inset, same location in 2005.

Marketing:
How Theater Owners Filled the Seats

Promoting the films at local theaters was done in a variety of ingenious ways. There were large newspaper advertisements designed to get the reader's attention. But, that was just the beginning. Theater operators hung advertisements on front doors of houses around town. They held contests and games that required attendance at the theater. They had drawings for money and prizes that required signing up for a chance to win.

Major studios provided promotional packages filled with posters and displays called "Ballyhoos" and scheduled personal appearances by their movie stars, especially the stars of the popular Westerns.

Personal Appearances

Harold Miller, a local Newberry resident, recounted being in the Newberry Opera House many years before and seeing cowboy movie star Tex Ritter leading his horse up the stairs to the theatre. "The horse was trained to walk up stairs," he said. "They also went to the junior high school and the horse walked up the stairs to get on the stage."

Typical Newspaper Advertisement
Reliance Theater - Orangeburg
January 1, 1937

Star of "Tarzan" to Appear in Person

Nelson Parker of Manning told us of a very exciting personal appearance he remembered. "It was advertised that one of the stars of the latest "Tarzan" picture would be appearing in person at the opening performance on Saturday. The house was packed. Everyone expected to see Johnny Weissmuller on stage. When the "star" was introduced, it was Cheetah! The children didn't seem to care and were thrilled to see the chimp. Cheetah would jump off the stage, run into the audience, and climb into the balcony, all to the screaming delight of the packed house."

Cheetah was as frequent a visitor at South Carolina movie theaters as Lash LaRue. We learned from Kent Daniels of Lake City, that Cheetah was actually an imposter. The chimp was owned by a man in Florence who rented him to any theater manager who asked. This chimp was often seen in Florence, waiting alone in the car for his owner. It was also reported that the chimp loved to smoke cigars.

Lash LaRue was Everywhere

Mr. Henry Clinkscales, who ran the local drug store in Belton, remembered, "Sometimes movie stars came to town to promote their films. When I was twelve or thirteen, Lash LaRue came to town. He rode his horse right down the aisle of the theater. He did whip tricks. He would get someone to hold a cigarette in their mouth and he'd cut it down with his whip. Then, if you bought a picture of him for fifty cents, he would autograph it. I didn't have fifty cents so I tore a popcorn box and he signed it. Gabby Hayes was here too."

Jimmy Lowe, at Belva's Flower Shop in Mount Pleasant, remembered the time Lash LaRue appeared in person at the American Theatre in downtown Charleston. "You got in free with the box-top from a package of Hadacol. My mother went to the Parkway Pharmacy, next to the Parkway Theater in Mount Pleasant, and bought a bottle of Hadacol. She said she hoped Lash LaRue never came back to Charleston because she wasn't going to buy another bottle of that awful tasting Hadacol."

Hadacol was a tonic advertised as a vitamin suppliment. It contained 12% alcohol "as a preservative" and was very popular during Prohibition because it was legal.

Gene Black remembered personal appearances in his home town of Kingstree. "Yeah, I remember going to the Anderson Theater. Lash LaRue was there in person. I met Don "Red" Berry, star of the 1940s' Republic serial, "The Adventures of Red Ryder." A lot of people were there.

We found a newspaper article in *The Times-Herald,* of Lake City, dated June 25, 1953, that indicated Lash LaRue saved the day at the local tobacco festival.

"Every businessman knows that the biggest day in the year for Lake City is when the chant of the tobacco auctioneer is heard the first time.

To help usher in this most important day, your local Chamber of Commerce sponsored the "Golden Leaf Jubilee." Plans called for the appearance of Lash LaRue, Smiley Burnette and his troop, an air show put on by planes from Shaw Air Force Base followed by a street dance that night.

Because of unforeseen circumstances, Smiley never did show up, but Lash LaRue took up the slack by taking part in the parade and putting on a wonderful exhibition in front of the Propst Theatre that night. The street dance atracted a huge throng."

Propst Theater - Lake City

Cash Night Drew Crowds

It was easy to get a crowd on Friday and Saturday nights. It was harder to fill the theater during the week. Theater owners promoted "Cash Night" or "Bank Night" on off-days.

A person would sign a book in the lobby beside a number. On "Cash Night" the theater manager would draw a number from a large drum on stage after the movie. The person who had signed by that number had about three minutes to come to the stage and claim their money.

Prizes were usually $100. If no one claimed the prize, it was increased to $150 and the drawing repeated the following week. This promotion not only helped the manager fill the theater on off nights but allowed him to run cheap films to a packed house.

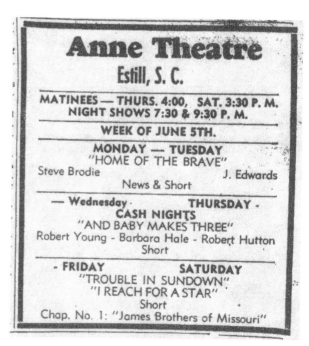

Anne Theater - Estill - Cash Nights were on Wednesday and Thursday in 1950.

The 1927 issue of *Film Yearbook* ran a feature article called "Practical Showmanship Ideas." The article gives promotional ideas for the theater manager to use in newspapers, lobbies, theater fronts, window displays, special showings and special stunts.

The section on special stunts is an insightful and humourous look at marketing in the 1920s. Theater managers continued to use ideas like this into the 1960s. Below are some quoted "stunts' that were recommended in the article.

Confidential Tip

Distribute small envelopes with this message printed on them: "Take my advice and don't go home tonight." On the inside is a slip reading: "Go to the (_____) Theater and see (_____)."

Thumb Print Contest

A Thumb Print Contest to find one most nearly resembling that of the star in feature. For three days prior to showing the newspaper prints a coupon bearing star's thumb print, and a place for the contestant's print. Those submitted are taken to the superintendent of police. Prizes awarded to the three first, and passes to others.

Free Taxi Ride

Taxi cabs to carry on front of their radiators large one-sheet card reading "Free ride to see (_____) at the (_____) Theater if it rains between 7 and 9 pm (on the opening night of picture). Nine cases out of ten, it doesn't rain and if it did, very few people would take advantage of the offer, but this great stunt will get everyone talking about this unique method of advertising.

Theater managers printed door hangers and hired young people to hang them on front doors of houses in the city. This door hanger promoted "Strange Interlude" released by Metro-Goldwyn-Mayer in 1932, starring Norma Shearer and Clark Gable.

This promotional tag encouraged patrons to see "Treasure Island" starring Wallace Beery and Jackie Cooper. If you brought the tag to the lobby, you could see if your key unlocked a treasure chest containing valuable prizes.

Ballyhoo

One of the more interesting ways to promote a movie was called the Ballyhoo. A Ballyhoo was a flamboyant decoration used at the theater entrance to draw attention to the movie. All of these Ballyhoos are from the Palmetto Theatre in Columbia.

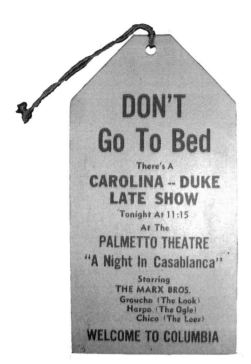

Tag for "A Night In Casablanca" with the Marx Brothers was designed for people attending the Duke vs. Carolina game in Columbia in 1946.

"Sweethearts" released by Twentieth Century Fox in 1938, starred Jeanette MacDonald and Nelson Eddy.

"Out West with the Hardy's" released in 1938 by Metro-Goldwyn-Mayer, starring Mickey Rooney.

Our profound thanks go to David Suggs of Blythewood for sharing examples of marketing pieces which were used under the direction of his father, Malcolm Samuel Suggs, City Manager of the seven Columbia theaters in the Wilby-Kincey Chain.

Window display at dime store promoted their Disney toys and "Dumbo" playing at Palmetto Theater.

Sidewalk Specialty

In this example of a Sidewalk Specialty, a "Jackass" sits atop a tall ladder in front of the Palmetto Theater to promote "Hellzapoppin" starring the comedy team of Olsen and Johnson. The sign on the ladder reads, "I may be a Jackass but I'm not coming down until Helzapoppin' with Olsen and Johnson opens." The film was released in 1941 by Universal Pictures.

When co-author Mark Tiedje was an usher at the Daytona Beach Theatre in the late 1950s, he was assigned to a "Sidewalk Specialty" called "The Box." He had to sit in a large closed box in front of the theater until someone walked by. Then he loudly scratched the sides and top and made the scariest, most fiendish noises he could. This was to promote the horror movie "The Fly" released by Twentieth Century Fox in 1958.

Sidewalk Specialty at the Palmetto Theater on North Main Street in Columbia in 1941

This uniformed usher is wearing a bright sash promoting the next attraction, "She Wore a Yellow Ribbon" starring John Wayne and Joanne Dru. The photograph was taken at the Palmetto Theater in Columbia in 1949.

LOCAL MOVIES
FILL THEATERS

One interesting promotional concept was the traveling filmmaker. Over the years, many of these men traveled from city to city filming local citizens, town officials, and merchants. They edited the scenes into a film about that city. Often, the soundtrack was prerecorded and written in such a way that it was generic and could be used for any city. Such is the case with the movie shot in Camden in 1946.

The title of the film is "My Home Town." That way, the same title could be used, no matter which town was being filmed. The title was usually followed by a shot of the town's "Welcome" sign, or a close-up of the town's name on the fire station. Local merchants paid the filmmaker to feature their businesses in the film.

Word spread quickly that a movie was being made in town. The film was developed and edited on the spot and shown at a local movie theater the next evening. Of course, this brought many people to the theater to see themselves on the screen.

We were very fortunate to acquire a copy of the Camden film from Gretchen Roepke, granddaughter of T. Lee Little, who ran the movie theater in Camden. Gretchen said her grandfather showed "My Home Town" before the feature film. On those evenings, the theater was always full.

There is a similar movie made in Anderson in 1926. However, this film follows a group of children around town, much like the "Our Gang Comedies" of the period. The film was sponsored by the Egyptian Theater of Anderson. Hundreds of kids showed up for the filming and are included in the film. Harry Osteen, who later ran movie theaters in Anderson, played a kid similar to "Spanky" from the "Little Rascal" movies.

Scenes from "My Home Town" showing the Camden Fire Department, women in a local dress shop, and children in front of the Palace Barber Shop.

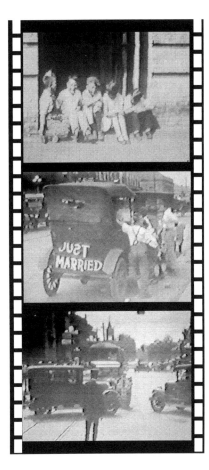

Scenes from Anderson's
"Our Gang Comedy" made in 1926.

The movie follows the "gang" as they throw a pie in a man's face, direct traffic, eat bananas, and catch a ride with a young married couple. No doubt the Egyptian Theater was full with children and their parents when the film was screened.

Many of these local films were made but few survive. We know of one filmed in Chesnee but have been unable to locate a copy. They were very popular then and are of great historical value now.

Besides films made to promote local business and theaters, crews from *Movietone News* and *Pathe News* traveled the country looking for good stories to show in theaters nationwide.

The Augusta Chronicle
March 24, 1929

Pathe to Picture Asparagus Fields

Blackville, SC, the cucumber capital of the South, was given additional prominence today when a Pathe News cameraman, Geo. W. Cook, shot some five or six hundred feet of film of the asparagus industry of the farm of Simon Brown's sons near Blackville.

Mr. Cook has been shooting films in and around Aiken in connection with the horse show, polo games and other tourist's activities there. Stanley Brown, manager of the Lyric Theatre, of Blackville, and a number of other theatres in this section prevailed upon Mr. Cook to visit his father's farm to make motion pictures of the actual cutting, picking and shipping of asparagus.

Seventy-eight attractive young ladies from Williston, Elko, Blackville, Denmark and other points were on hand dressed as farmerettes, all attired in overalls. Most of these were high school girls and were under the direction, in addition to Mr. Cook and Mr. Brown, of Col. Harry Calhoun of Denmark.

The title of the film that will be shown throughout the nation next week in Pathe News will be "How the Progressive Green Grass Growers Association Does Things."

Prominent asparagus growers from this section and sales representatives from Boston, New York, and elsewhere, were on hand to witness the shooting which brought out a large crowd of local citizens.

Hollywood Comes to Georgetown

On November 6, 1923, a special train arrived in Georgetown. The four Pullman cars carried movie stars and a crew from Paramount Pictures. They had come to Georgetown to make a movie. An enthusiastic group of townspeople crowded the depot to greet the 65 members of the company.

The Georgetown Times reported, "Headed by Mayor J.W. Wingate, a delegation consisting of Mr. A.G. Trenholm, who has taken great interest in the filming of the picture at Georgetown, Mr. F.M. Brickman, President of the Merchants Association, President F.A. Bell, of the Chamber of Commerce, and others, met the celebrities as they stepped from the train and after delivering a brief expression of welcome and a hearty handshake, dispatched them to the quarters selected among the different homes of the city, where they will be entertained during their stay here."

The movie was "Pied Piper Malone" written by Booth Tarkington. It is a sentimental story of a young man in love with a pretty school teacher.

The story is set in a New England town called "Oldport." Jack Malone (played by Thomas Meighan) longs for a life at sea but he loves school teacher, Patty Thomas (played by Lois Wilson). Jack is accused of causing the loss of a ship. Most everyone in town rejects him. Only Patty and the school children believe he is innocent. He is vindicated. Patty pledges her love as he sails away on the ship his family bought for him.

The names of the stars of "Pied Piper Malone" are almost unknown to us today, but they were famous in 1923. Thomas Meighan was six feet tall, with black hair and brown eyes, and a major star for Paramount.

Lois Wilson is best remembered as Shirley Temple's mother in the 1934 film, "Bright Eyes." When Wilson came to Georgetown in 1923, she was a serene beauty with expressive eyes and one of Paramount's biggest stars.

Scenes from
"Pied Piper Malone"
made by
Paramount Pictures in
Georgetown in 1924.

"PIED PIPER MALONE"

Thomas Meighan

Lois Wilson

Released Feb 4, 1924

Mildred Higgins (seated)
with her daughters Karen and Loril

Among the cast were several children, known then as "starlets." They played the principal children's roles in the movie. The story required a large number of children to follow the hero as scenes were filmed around town. Local school children were chosen as "extras" for the film.

We interviewed Mrs. Mildred Higgins in July, 2005. She remembered when Hollywood came to Georgetown. Together with Mrs. Higgins' exciting memories, local newspaper accounts, and information from the Georgetown County Museum and international film archives, we began to piece together the story.

Mrs. Higgins recalled the day the director came to her school. "On the first or second day that they were here, several of the executives came to the school and explained to the principal how they planned to use the Georgetown children in the movie.

We were brought out to the front of the school building and asked to stand quietly on the steps. The director had someone to choose boys and girls for the scenes to be shot that day. He pointed and said, "You, you, and you." I was so surprised and elated when I was selected. I think I got picked because of my red hair.

The director told the children who were not selected that some of them would be used at another time, and they were. We were excused from school that day and told to go with the movie crew.

We marched to the Court House on Prince and Screven Streets. Directions were given and, after a little adjusting of collars and sashes and hair brushing, we swarmed around the hero of the story, taking our cues from the real little actors. Soon we were "acting" the best we knew how.

Inside the Court House, we stood in the doorway and listened to a court session going on. We did what the director told us to do. There was a lot of jumping and hand clapping and joyful gestures. We thought we were movie stars.

It was fascinating to watch those young starlets perform. I remember a little boy named Tommy and one little curly-haired blond who could turn on the tears at the drop of a hat.

The Episcopal Church, the Masonic Temple, the Baltimore Steamship Company, the Front Street docks (where the Gulf Marina now stands) were some of the places for scenes. The old Moose Lodge, which used to be the beautiful home of the Kaminski family, was the home of the Malone family in the movie. The Joseph Schenk home was used as the home of the heroine in the film.

The Winyah Indigo Society Hall, the Winyah School, the Wigwam Ice Cream Parlor, on the corner of Front and Screven Streets, and many other Front Street stores were used. There were scenes laid at many places on the waterfront as the hero went away to sea and returned.

There were many scenes on other days, happy ones and sad ones, and we never grew tired of the proceedings. Every day it was something new. Best of all was pay-day. We were lined up at the waterfront and handed crisp one-dollar bills – brand new money.

I think I had about twelve dollars in all. I felt like a millionaire because I had never had that much money in all of my ten years! I used some of it to buy Christmas presents. What luxury!"

When the members of the company were not shooting scenes they enjoyed the hospitality of the people of Georgetown. The cast attended various churches and went sightseeing on the water and to the many interesting old rice plantations. The weather was described as "bright and crisp, perfect condition for taking pictures for the screen."

The Georgetown Chamber of Commerce held a reception and dance to honor the cast and crew of "Pied Piper Malone" at the historical Winyah Indigo Society Hall on Friday, November 16, 1923. Splendid music was donated by the Elks' Band.

Thomas Meighan said that because of the courtesies and kindness of the people of Georgetown he wanted them to capitalize on their being in town. He offered the services of the entire cast to perform in a benefit entertainment to raise money for an appropriate charity.

On Friday night, November 23, a benefit performance was given at the Winyah School Auditorium. In all, $700 was raised for the Health Fund of the Civic League. Mrs. J.S. Higgins, President of the Civic League received the money for the specific purpose of providing for the undernourished children of the Public Schools.

After three weeks of almost perfect weather the movie company completed their filming in Georgetown and prepared to leave for New York. A large crowd gathered at the depot to say goodbye.

In February, 1924, "Pied Piper Malone" played to packed performances at the Princess Theatre on Front Street. The newspaper reported that, "Georgetonians will be given the opportunity to see themselves as well as a number of their friends and children in this big picture. The school children hold a prominent part throughout the outdoor scenes and it is expected that the Princess Theatre will have a record attendance."

Mrs. Mildred Higgins said, "Being in 'Pied Piper Malone' was a once-in-a-lifetime thrill, but seeing the movie when it was shown on the screen was icing on the cake. Recognizing ourselves and our friends filled us with glee, and we were happy to see the movie starlets again on the screen if not in person."

After interviewing Mrs. Higgins, we thought how wonderful it would be if she could see the film again. We did a little research and found that, of the 590 films made in the United States in 1923, only 135 are known to exist today. Frank Thompson's book "Lost Films" listed "Pied Piper Malone" as one of those films that had been lost.

We mentioned this to Pat Doyle, President of the Georgetown County Historical Society. She said a member of the society had located a copy of the film in Russia but was unable to contact anyone there about it. We contacted Jared Case at the George Eastman House and he confirmed that Russia did have a copy of the film.

We went online and found an email address for the Gosfilmofond Archives in Moscow. We sent a request for "Pied Piper Malone." Weeks later, we had about given up when we received an email from Valerij Bosenko, stating that the film was at Gosfilmofond. She referred us to Sonia Demetrieva at Technovid, a Russian film lab. Another couple of weeks went by and we heard from Sonia. She simply asked if we preferred to receive a copy of the film on videotape or DVD. We were stunned!

The Georgetown Historical Society raised the $1,017 dollars to have the Russian film lab pull the original film print from the vault, clean it, and make a transfer to DVD. After a complicated international money transfer, we waited nervously for the DVD to arrive.

When it did arrive, it was in the European format and it had to be transferred again into the North American DVD format. Then, we discovered that the Russians had changed the inter-titles from English to Russian. We hadn't anticipated that.

A former translator for the Library of Congress, Boris Buhun-Chudynev, translated the 132 Russian inter-titles back into English. Marty Tennant, the PC Doctor in Georgetown, carefully replaced all 132 inter-titles. The historical society began plans to have a "re-premiere" of the film.

On Saturday, March 25, 2006, the silent film "Pied Piper Malone" was shown again in Georgetown after eighty-two years. It was shown at the Strand Theater at 710 Front Street. That is the location of the old Princess Theater where the film was first shown in Georgetown in 1924.

The street was lined with cheering people. Vintage cars pulled up with "movie stars" while photographers took pictures for newspapers and television. Cameras flashed as the honored guests walked the red carpet to see the restored print.

Attending the matinee were Mildred Higgins, Mamie Dalzell, Joyce McLeod, Frankie Tyson, and Margaret Tyson, who appeared as extras in the film. They were escorted by Richard Clerc, whose mother, now deceased, also appeared in the film.

Logan Young, a talented grandson of Mrs. Higgins, and a music major at the University of South Carolina, provided an original musical score to accompany the movie.

A reception at the home of Sallie and Tom Gillespie was the perfect ending for this unforgettable event, especially because this house was used in the film.

Georgetown women who played children in the 1924 Paramount Pictures movie "Pied Piper Malone" arrive for screening of the film in 2006.

THEATER OWNERS AND OPERATORS

In the era of single-screen movie theaters, most of them were owned and operated by local people. It was sometimes a family business that extended over generations. We were able to record some of this rich history. Some of it continues to elude us.

One of the first towns we visited when we began our research was Elloree, South Carolina. We walked along Cleveland Street asking local shop owners if they remembered a movie theater in Elloree. One woman told us, "Go ask at the antique shop in the old Hall's five and dime store. They'll know."

Delores Wright who ran the antique shop told us, "I don't think the theatre was in this building. It was built in 1902. Mr. Hall started the five and dime store here in 1938. There is a small area upstairs that has what looks to be a small stage at one end."

"This was once the telephone exchange for Elloree. The switchboard was upstairs. The windows faced the street." She laughed and said, "Someone might call and ask to speak to so-and-so. The telephone operator would look out the window and say, "Won't do any good. She's out in her back yard right now."

Delores told us to ask at the antique store down the street. There we met Nancy Felkel who did remember the Playland Theatre. "It was across the street where that empty lot is next to the radio repair shop," she said. "It was owned by Dr. Green, a local physician, who had his office in the back of the drug store."

Nancy said we should talk to Kit Brandenburg in the radio repair shop. "He's always lived here," she said.

Kit told us the Playland Theater had been upstairs over Hall's five and dime store for a short time. "Then," he said, "Dr. J.T. Green, Sr., built a building next door to this shop and moved the Playland into it." He told us we should contact Dr. Green's son. "He lives in St. George. His father also owned theaters in Branchville, New Ellenton and St. George."

Now we knew there was more than one of the Green family in the movie theater business. The primary materials we relied on for information, such as theater directories, fire insurance maps, and newspaper advertisements rarely mentioned the names of local theater owners.

Most of what we learned about the theater owners and operators came from people we talked with as we traveled from city to city. Sometimes, the unofficial town historian would tell us who built or owned the local theater. Occasionally, we would encounter a relative who was excited to relate their family's movie theater involvement.

While our account of local men and women who ran movie theaters in South Carolina is far from complete, it does provide a good idea of how unique, ambitious, and dedicated these people were. They filled a need by providing entertainment to those all across the state who wanted to go the the movies.

THE GREEN/GREENE FAMILY

Some months after our trip to Elloree, we talked to Dr. Green's grandson on the phone. J.T. Green, III, recalled a time when his family operated movie theatres in several towns across South Carolina.

"My father (J.T. Green, Jr. 1913-2005) owned theatres in Branchville, St. George, Erhardt, and New Ellenton. He had two brothers who owned theatres in Johnston, Williston, Yemassee, and Hardeville.

Most of the movie places my family owned were drive-ins. We had drive-ins in Erhardt, Yemasse, and Hardeville. The Skyline Drive-in, in New Ellenton, was the first drive-in with a paved black-top parking area. It could hold 300 cars. The drive-in in St. George was destroyed by Hurricane Gracie on September 29, 1959. Ticket sales had been slow anyway because of television so my father didn't bother to rebuild."

It was awhile before we connected with another member of the Green family. Bill Greene not only gave us much information on the theaters his family owned, but provided us with many photographs.

Bill recalled, "My father built the drive-in in Yemassee and operated it for a couple of years. That would've been in the 1950s, during which time we also operated drive-ins in Hardeeville and Ridgeland.

My father took over operation of the Ridgeland drive-in from the original owners, John Hubbard & Willie Sauls.

A childhood memory from the Hardeeville drive-in is that my older sister and I, both of us pre-schoolers, learned our ABC's and numerals from our parents holding up the large wooden cut-outs of letters and numbers which were used on the marquee. Those were some pretty hefty flash-cards!

Over the years I've often thought that my sister and I got a pretty good "head start" education from watching all those movies during the early 1950s, especially since there was no television in our area at the time."

Foul Smell Clears Ediso Theater

J.T. Green, operated the Edisto Theater in Branchville, which opened in 1937. It was a small wood frame building. It had a wood-stove for what little heat was needed. J.T. Green, Jr. recalled one memorable evening at the Edisto Theater when he was a young boy.

"One Halloween, my father organized a "Spook Show" at the theater, which meant, he exhibited some very scary movies. It was a chilly night and the wood-stove was being used. It threw out too much light to see the movie, so he asked me to go backstage behind the screen where he always kept buckets of water.

I brought a nearly-full bucket and poured some water on the fire in the stove to dowse it a little. The stove hissed and let out a big cloud of steam. It also let out such a foul smell that it cleared the theater. Because it was a cold night and the theater had no restrooms, some of the young boys had sneaked behind the screen and peed in the water bucket backstage."

The Green Family: Standing: W.F. Greene
Seated left to right: J.C. "Coty" Greene, J.T. Green, Jr., and Dr. J.T. Green, Sr.

The Augusta Chronicle
March 24, 1944

Elloree Man Buys Williston Theatre

It has been announced that Dr. J.T. Greene, of Elloree, has recently purchased the Williston Theatre. The theatre, formerly owned and operated by Mrs. Elizabeth Vanderburgh for a number of years was sold to Dr. Greene several months ago so that she could join her husband who is a member of the armed forces.

Mrs. Myrtle Starnes, of Williston, new manager of the theatre, began her work this week.

Williston Theater
Williston, SC

This theater was owned and operated by William (Bill) and Dotty Greene. It had 250 seats. The photograph is from around 1947

THE ABRAMS BROTHERS

From an interview with
Mrs. Helmer Abrams
May 10, 2005

The Abrams brothers, Morris, Carroll, Sidney and Helmer, were reared in the theaters in Lake City as well as in Georgetown. Morris, the oldest brother, worked for a man, I believe his name was Mr. Cook, who had a theater.

All the boys were very bright, particularly Morris. He was working in the theatre and going to school. His father told him, either go to school or work in the theater, you can't do both. He began working in the theater in Lake City full time.

I've heard my husband, Helmer, tell this story many times. When the boxing matches came on over the radio, he would listen to the match to find out how it was going and then he would run down and tell his brother Morris, who would project on the screen how the boxing match was going.

During the depths of the depression, Morris somehow obtained the theater. The next older brother was Carroll. He finished the University of South Carolina and then he and Engle Hazzard came to Georgetown and started a bank called the Georgetown Cash Depository.

At that time, Morris sold the theater in Lake City. About twenty years ago, my husband and I went to an affair in Lake City. The place had changed so much we couldn't tell where we were. My husband stopped the car and asked a black man if he knew where the Haskels lived. The fellow said, "Ain't you one of the Abrams brothers?" It was a man named Princey who had worked for Morris at the theater in Lake City.

After Carroll opened up the bank, Morris, Helmer, and their mother came from Lake City to Georgetown. The other brother, Sidney, was entering the University of South Carolina. Helmer entered high school in Georgetown. I believe Morris opened the Palace Theater first. Then they opened the Strand. Morris ran both theaters in Georgetown and one in Andrews.

Every child went to the movie theater on a Saturday. It was a wonderful place to leave your children at that time. One time, my son was going to the movies on a Saturday and, naturally, they were all throwing popcorn boxes and God knows what else. Morris and Lillian had no children. Morris was standing in the back of the theatre and he saw the popcorn boxes flying and he cut the movie off.

He went down front and said, "The next one that throws a popcorn box will never be allowed to come in this theatre again!" He stood in the back for awhile and of course, the popcorn boxes started flying again. Well, Morris saw the kid who threw the first one in the air and he went down the aisle and yanked this boy up by the scruff of his neck and it was my son, Morris' nephew!

The brothers opened two drive-ins, one in Andrews and one in Georgetown. Morris became ill and had to have a very serious operation in Charleston. Carroll closed the theaters while Morris was down in Charleston. Morris retired after that.

Carroll sold the Palace Theater to the First Citizens Bank. Morris' widow, Lillian Abrams, sold the Strand Theater to community theatre group.

STILL STANDING: NEW USES FOR OLD THEATERS

There are many of the old single-screen movie theaters still standing in cities and towns across South Carolina. We covered some of them earlier in this book. These are some others that still find useful service in their communities but were not included in the earlier text.

Clemson Theater - Clemson
Sports Shop

Little Theater - Bamberg
Community Theater

Andrews Theater - Andrews
Equipment Rental Store

Lakeview Theater - Lakeview
Beauty Shop

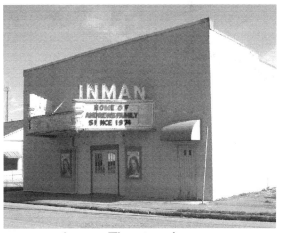

Inman Theater - Inman
Church

New Theater - Holly Hill
Vacant

Falls Theater - Great Falls
806 Dearborn St.

(Falls Theater) Located in the town of Great Falls, the Republic Theater was built by Republic Cotton Mills in 1921-1922. In 1917 Republic Cotton Mills commissioned J.E. Serrine and Company, a Greenville, South Carolina architectural firm, to complete plans and specifications for the theater. The theater closed in 1974. Listed in the National Register November 25, 1980.

Anderson Theater - Mullins
Now Anderson Center
houses 14 apartments since 2003.

St. Stephen Theater - St. Stephen
Now a church

About the Lists

The following pages contain two lists of theaters. We begin with single-screen movie theaters and continue with drive-ins. When we began researching the theater history of South Carolina, the first challenge was to identify all of the theaters in every city and town across the state. We wanted to include every theater, from the earliest to the present. Someone is certain to point out theaters we missed. We consulted two reliable references, *The Film Daily Yearbook of Motion Pictures*, 1945, 1961 and 1965 editions, and *The Julius Cahn and Gus Hill Theatrical Guide and Moving Picture Directory* from the years 1908, 1913, and 1921. These two sources provided our preliminary list.

To expand our listings, we consulted various digital collections of Sanborn Maps. The Sanborn Company produced maps, primarily to assess fire insurance liability, in about 12,000 U.S. cities from 1867 to 2007. Movie theaters used nitrate film in the early days. This material was highly combustible and often caught fire in the projector. The Sanborn Maps usually highlight movie theaters of this period due to their hazardous nature.

The fourth most valuable source material was newspapers on microfilm. Most of these have not been digitized and are available in limited locations. We traveled to libraries around the state and spent countless hours viewing reels of microfilm looking for local movie advertisements, stories about new theater construction, and stories about sudden destructive theater fires or the demolition of old theaters. The old newspaper stories provided much broader information than the directories and maps.

We talked to local people. That not only provided the most pleasant of our research experiences, but often brought surprising results. One woman told us that her mother had spoken of a local theater in the small community of Cottageville. When we visited Cottageville, no one seemed to know anything about a local theater. No one remembered there being a theater in there. Then, we were directed to one of the older residents of the town, Mrs. Cockfield. She told us her father had opened the small movie theater there in 1941. This movie theater had not surfaced in the directories, maps, or newspaper articles. But, we visited the building and found traces of the theater.

We have limited our first list to single screen movie theaters. We did not always include the old Opera Houses. They often exhibited movies, but were primarily used for live stage performances. We did include combo-houses. These were a combination of vaudeville and motion picture theaters.

The list of drive-in movie theaters was more difficult to create. Drive-ins were listed in some of the *Film Daily Yearbook* volumes, but little information was given. Many of the names of drive-ins came from our hours spent in front of the microfilm viewers, reading local newspapers. We were sometimes contacted by local residents through our website. We hope we included your favorite drive-in on our list. We expecially thank Bill Green for the information and photographs of the drive-ins operated by his family.

SOUTH CAROLINA THEATERS

The following list of theaters in South Carolina is as inclusive as we can make it. There will, no doubt, be theaters we missed. The cities are listed alphabetically. We did not list the theaters alphabetically by name, nor did we attempt to list them chronologically. We have tried to list dates of operation and location, but this information varies according to our sources. We have also indicated if a theater has been included in the Nation Register of Historic Places (NRHP).

Theatre	Location	Seats	Note
Abbeville			
Abbeville Opera House	100 Court Square	800	NRHP
Mills		200	(1927) Film Yearbook
Community		200	(1927) Film Yearbook
Aiken			
Aiken			
Princess			
New Colored			African American
Patricia		700	
Rosemary			
Cinema			
Alcolu			
Alcolu	US Hwy 521	200	
Allendale			
Pastime		250	(1927) Film Yearbook
Carolina		300	WH Rentz, mgr (1920)
Anderson			
Anderson Opera House			1905-1914
Palace Electric	114 N. Main St.		1907-1914
Park	Off E. River St.		1907-1911
Airdrome	210 N. Main St.		1909-1909
Knickerbocker	E. Whitner St.		1911-1912
Lyric	133 N. Main St.		1911-1913
Palmetto	133 N. Main St.		1914-1918
Liberty	133 N. Main St.	300	1918-1926
Egyptian	133 N. Main St.		1926-1932
Hudinell	404 S. Main St.		1913-1916
Garrick			1915-1915
Paramount	S. Main St.		1915-1915
Carolina	201 N. Main St.	400	1932-1957

Theatre	Location	Seats	Note
Anderson (continued)			
Anderson	204 W. Whitner St.	800	1915-1924
Garden	204 W. Whitner St.	300	1924-1931
Criterion	204 W. Whitner St.	500	1931-1960
Lyrie		274	
State	131 E. Whitner St.	1000	1939-1972
ACT	131 E. Whitner St.		NRHP
Strand	126 N. Main St.	600	1920-1945
Center	126 N. Main St.		1946-1955
Victor	113 W. Church St.	200	1920-1923 African American
Bijou	214 S. Main St.		1913-1920 (Burned)
Imperial	214 S. Main St.	700	1921-1928
Pastime	129 Queen St.		1927-1930
Ritz	114 E. Church St.		1931-1941
Osteen	613 N. Main St.		1955-1994
Belvedere	3130 N. Main St	200	1969-1994
Andrews			
Bijou			(1921) Cahn and Hill
Majestic			(1921) Cahn and Hill
Princess		950	(1921) Cahn and Hill
Andrews		225	
Bamberg			
La Victory			(1921) Cahn and Hill
Lyric			(1921) Cahn and Hill
Little	160 N. Main St.	300	
Barnwell			
Woodland			(1921) Cahn and Hill
Vamp		350	(1927) Film Yearbook
Ritz		300	
Batesburg			
Grand			(1921) Cahn and Hill
Carolina		300	Sam Bogo, mgr (1938)
Bath			
Aiken County Stores		300	
Beaufort			
Breeze	924 Bay Street	300	
Palm		300	

Theatre	Location	Seats	Note
Belton			
Pastime			(1921) Cahn and Hill
Amuzu		250	(1927) Film Yearbook
Belton	226 Belton Square	360	
Virginia		260	
Joy			
Bennettsville			
Alamo			(1921) Cahn and Hill
Pastime		200	(1921) Cahn and Hill
Playhouse	106 Clyde St.	750	(1921) Cahn and Hill
Garden	106 Clyde St.	750	Formerly Playhouse
Carolina	106 Clyde St.	400	Formerly Garden
Cinema	106 Clyde St.	400	Formerly Carolina
Princess	234 E. Main St.		
Lincoln	120 W. Market St.	250	African American
Palace			African American
Bishopville			
Opera House			(1921) Cahn and Hill
Ackerman		300	(1927) Film Yearbook
Garden		250	(1927) Film Yearbook
Lyric	N. Main St.	300	
Andrews	221 N. Main St.		
Harper	221 N. Main St.		Formerly Andrews
Blacksburg			
Opera House		150	D.A. Gold, mgr
Star		300	Opened 1902
Broadway		200	(1927) Film Yearbook
State		350	
Blackville			
Lyric		300	Stanley Brown, mgr (1929)
Branchville			
Majestic		150	(1927) Film Yearbook
Edisto		200	
Buffalo			
Buffalo		350	
Calhoun Falls			
Mazda		300	

Theatre	Location	Seats	Note
Camden			
Opera House			L.A. McDowell, mgr
Majestic		450	
Lincoln		200	(1927) Film Yearbook
Camden		400	T. Lee Little, mgr
Haigler		500	
Little	506 E. DeKalb St.	1000	
Central			
Central		200	
Issaqueena		200	(1927) Film Yearbook
Charleston			
Academy of Music	225 King St.	800	1869-1931
Theatorium	321 King St.	114	1907-1908
Pastime	282 King St.		
Wonderland	249 King St.		1907- ?
Edisonia	263 King St.		
Idle Hour			1908
Majestic	343 King St.	300	1908-1950
Cameo	343 King St.		1950-1950, Torn down 1951
New Theatorium	King St.		
Airdome	Hampton Park		1907
Bon Air Park	368 King St.		1907
Victoria	84 Society St.	900	1911-1918
Victory	84 Society St.	900	1918-1946
Princess	304 King St.	800	1913- ?
Lyric	348 King St.		1909-1928 C.H. May, mgr
Elco	549 King St	300	A.W. Petit, mgr (1920)
Uno	368 King St.		1913-1915
Fairyland	348 King St.		1908-1909
Dixieland	616 King St.		1913- ? African American
Dreamland	158 King St.		1907
Maceo	422 King St.		1911- ?
Crescent	617 King St.		1913-1914
Orpheum	424 King St.		
Colonial	372 King St.		
Carolina	399 King St.	400	1932-1933
Dock Street	135 Church St.		
Garden	371 King St.		1918-2004
Lincoln	601 King St.	450	African American
Gloria	331 King St.	1000	Now Sottile Theatre
Milo	566 King St.		1921-1923
Charleston	566 King St.		1924-1931

Theatre	Location	Seats	Note
Charleston (continued)			
Palace	566 King St.		1931-1957, Torn down 1968
Riviera	225 King St.	914	1939-1983
American	343 King St.	900	1942-present
Arcade	5 Liberty St.		1948-2003
Ashley	Hwy 61 and Hwy 17		1950- ?
Terrace	Maybank Hwy		
Pictorium	294 King St.		1907
Cheraw			
Lyric		500	J.O. Hall, mgr (1920)
Cheraw 500		300	
Chesnee			
Colonial		119	
Star		300	
Chester			
Dreamland		400	(1921) Cahn and Hill
City		450	
Chester		450	(1938) Powell & Sipe
Powell		400	(1938) Powell & Sipe
Palmetto			
Chesterfield			
Chesterfield		300	
Clemson			
Clemson			
Clinton			
Gem		300	(1927) Film Yearbook
Broadway		300	
Casino		300	
Clio			
Edens Opera House			
Marlboro			
Clover			
Pleasu		225	(1927) Film Yearbook
Carolina		294	

Theatre	Location	Seats	Note
Columbia			
Columbia Opera House	Main & Gervais Sts.		
Columbia	Main & Gervais Sts.	1600	Formerly Columbia O.H.
Carolina	Main & Gervais Sts.	500	1931-1939 Formerly Columbia
Imperial		782	(1927) Film Yearbook
Palmetto		1600	1937-1979, Site of Imperial
Lincoln		782	(1927) Film Yearbook
Lyric			
Grand			
Ideal		700	
Ritz		870	1928-1980
Broadway		600	L.T. Lester, Jr., mgr (1921)
Rialto		385	L.T. Lester, Jr., mgr (1921)
Pastime			
Rivoli		800	L.T. Lester, Jr., mgr (1921)
Majestic			
Dreamland			
Rex			
Strand			1936-1958
Capitol		350	African American
Camp Jackson			Military Theater
Carolina (new)			1941-1983
Carver	1519 Harden St.	400	African American
Community House		300	
Five Points	632 Harden St.	600	
Royal		300	African American
State	1607 N. Main St.		1936-1961
Fox	1607 N. Main St.		1962-1987
Miracle			1968-1979
Jefferson Square	1801 N. Main St.	600	1970-1993
Richland Mall	Forest Dr. & Beltline	750	
Nickelodeon	937 S. Main St.		
Conway			
Casino			
Pastime		350	(1921) Cahn and Hill
Carolina		500	
Hillside			African American
Holliday		650	
Cottageville			
Cottageville			
Cowpens			
Gem		300	

Theatre	Location	Seats	Note
Darlington			
Bijou			
The Blue Mouse			
Mirror			
Pastime			
Alamo			(1921) Cahn and Hill
Dreamland			
Liberty		800	G.W. Hendrickson, mgr (1921)
Rex		400	
Carolina			
Darlington			
Denmark			
Lyric			(1921) Cahn and Hill
Arcadia		300	(1927) Film Yearbook
Dulamae			
Dane			Formerly Dulamae
Dillon			
Everybody's	Railroad Avenue	300	Torn down 1934
Broadway	West Main St.	300	
Dillon	114 N MacArthur Ave	450	Site of Everybody's
Easley			
Pastime			
Easley		100	W.C. Garrett, mgr (1921)
Avalon	Main St.	400	
Avalon	N. Pendleton St.		African American
Lyric		300	Phelps Sasseen, mgr (1921)
Colony			1948-2004
Edgefield			
Pastime			
Edgefield			(1921) Cahn and Hill
Towne		200	
Ellenton			
Ellenton		150	
(Town relocated. Site of town became Savannah Nuclear Site)			
Elloree			
Bluebird		200	(1927) Film Yearbook
Playland		300	Torn down in the 1960's

Theatre	Location	Seats	Note
Enoree			
Enoree		200	
Estill			
Imperial		150	(1927) Film Yearbook
Anne			
Estill		300	
Fairfax			
Pal		300	
Florence			
City Auditorium			Mr. Schnibben, mgr (1921)
Elite			African American-1910-1920
Imperial			(1921) Cahn and Hill
Liberty			(1921) Cahn and Hill
Opera House		700	
O'Dowd		750	J.M. OlDowd, mgr (1921)
Carolina		750	
Colonial		750	
Lincoln		300	African American
Roxy		300	
State		300	
Fort Mill			
Majestic	204 Main St.	200	NRHP
Center	100 Main St		Stewart & Everett, FDY 1965
Fountain Inn			
Liberty		250	(1921) Cahn and Hill
Essay		300	
Gaffney			
Star	402 N. Limestone	300	(1908) Sanborn Map
Strand	406 N. Limestone	500	(1921) Cahn and Hill
Cherokee	302 N. Limestone	517	(1938) Powell & Sipe
Capri	302 N. Limestone	300	Formerly Cherokee
Hamrick	306 N. Limestone	500	Gone
Georgetown			
Electric	810 Front St.		1908-1912
Air Dome	718 Front St.		1909-1914
Peerless	710 Front St.		1914-1940
Princess	638 Front St.	350	1914-1927

Theatre	Location	Seats	Note
Georgetown (continued)			
Palmetto	109 King St.	300	1920-1936
Palace	726 Front St.	350	1936-1968
Strand	710 Front St.	546	1941- Present, Site of Peerless
Granitville			
Granitville		250	
Great Falls			
Falls	806 Dearborn St.		
Republic	806 Dearborn St.	450	NRHP
Greenville			
Grand Opera House	202 W. Coffee St		
Bijou	206 N. Main St.	400	(1921) Cahn and Hill
Casino	228 N. Main St.	425	(1921) Cahn and Hill
Garing	215 N. Main St.	700	(1921) Cahn and Hill
Majestic	310 N. Main St.	500	
Rialto	124 N. Main St.	300	(1927) Film Yearbook
Egyptian		500	(1927) Film Yearbook
Knights of Columbus		300	(1921) Cahn and Hill
Strand			(1921) Cahn and Hill
Branwood		500	
Carolina	310 N. Main St.	500	Site of Majestic
Center		800	
Liberty		300	African American
Lyric			
Paris		500	
Ritz		450	
Roxy			Formerly Ritz
Rivoli		800	
Fox			Formerly Rivoli
Roosevelt		400	
Greenwood			
Bijou		250	(1927) Film Yearbook
Liberty		430	W.A. Bozers, mgr (1921)
Lyric		300	(1927) Film Yearbook
Pastime		350	(1927) Film Yearbook
Princess		200	(1927) Film Yearbook
Carolina		800	
Ritz		400	
State		1000	

Theatre	Location	Seats	Note
Greer			
Grand		400	
Ideal		250	(1927) Film Yearbook
Rialto		250	
Greer			Stewart & Everett, FDY 1965
Hampton			
Palmetto	108 Lee Ave.	200	Opened August 12, 1946
Hartsville			
Center	212 N Fifth St	700	
Temple		260	
Berry	118 West Carolina		
Hemmingway			
Amuzu		250	(1927) Film Yearbook
Anderson	110 Main St.	466	Anderson Theater Company
Holly Hill			
New	Old State Rd	200	
Honea Path			
Princess	107 S. Main St.	450	(1921) Cahn and Hill
Lyric		300	
Inman			
Amuzu		250	
Inman			
Iva			
Iva		250	
Joanna			
Gold			
Johnsonville			
Ritz		250	
Princess		450	(1927) Film Yearbook
Johnston			
Liberty		250	

Theatre	Location	Seats	Note
Kershaw			
Kershaw		175	
Pastime		250	(1927) Film Yearbook
State		300	
Kingstree			
Academy		250	C.J. Thompson, mgr (1921)
Unana			
Anderson		400	Anderson Theater Co
Lake City			
New		400	(1927) Film Yearbook
Ritz		350	
Propst			
Lakeview			
Lakeview		300	
Lancaster			
Star		275	(1921) Cahn and Hill
Imperial		400	
Midway		550	
Parr		500	
Landrum			
Civic		225	
Langley			
Aiken County Stores		300	
Latta			
Latta 300			
Laurens			
Opera House		300	(1927) Film Yearbook
Idle Hour	107 E. Laurens St.		A.S. Perry, mgr
Princess		300	W.M. Switzer, mgr (1921)
Garlington		200	(1927) Film Yearbook
Liberty		150	(1927) Film Yearbook
Capitol		400	
Echo		300	
Lexington			
Carolina		300	

Theatre	Location	Seats	Note
Liberty			
Roxy		300	
Lockhart			
Lockhart		250	
Loris			
State		300	Anderson Theater Co
Lyman			
Lyman		350	
McColl			
Everybody's		300	D.C. Malay, mgr (1921)
Carolina		300	
McColl		250	
McCormick			
Dixie		200	(1927) Film Yearbook
Hollywood		200	
Manning			
Hollywood		250	
Pastime		300	(1921) Cahn and Hill
Parkhill			
Marion			
Rainbow	307 N. Main St.	638	(1921) Cahn and Hill
Marion			
Colored		300	D.K. Davis, mgr (1921)
Idle Hour		500	D.K. Davis, mgr (1921)
Opera House		450	Crawford & Oakerson, mgrs
Moncks Corner			
Berkeley		375	
Moncks Corner			
Mount Pleasant			
Parkway	Coleman Blvd		
Mullins			
Kirbys		450	(1927) Film Yearbook
Peoples			(1927) Film Yearbook
Anderson	143 N. Main St.	400	Anderson Theater Co

Theatre	Location	Seats	Note
Myrtle Beach			
Broadway		300	
Gloria		500	
Rivoli		1078	Opened 1958
Camelot			
Gayety			
Newberry			
Newberry Opera House	Boyce & Nance Sts	600	NRHP
Imperial		400	(1927) Film Yearbook
Ritz		300	
Wells		400	burned down 1950s
New Brookland			
Dixie		300	
New Ellenton			
Virma			
Ninety-Six			
Ideal		200	(1927) Film Yearbook
Star			Sidney McNeill, owner 1933-1975
Gloria		400	
North			
Rex		150	(1927) Film Yearbook
Maxlyn		250	
New		250	
North Augusta			
Marrh			
Carolina			Formerly Marrh
North Charleston			
Dixie		400	
Port		400	
Fox			
North Myrtle Beach			
Ocean Drive	209 Main St.		Anderson Theater Co.
Colonial			Anderson Theater Co.
Playhouse	212 24th Ave.		
Surf	225 Main St.		

Theatre	Location	Seats	Note
Olar			
Olar		150	(1927) Film Yearbook
Orangeburg			
Academy of Music		800	J. B. Seignious, mgr (1921)
Garden			(1927) Film Yearbook
Star			
Blue Bird		225	J. Harlod Ziegler, mgr (1921)
Palmetto		200	African American
Carolina		1000	
Edisto		500	Now Bluebird on Russell St
Reliance		350	J. Harlod Ziegler, mgr (1921)
State		400	
Pacolet Mills			
Pacolet Mills (YMCA)		300	(1921) Cahn and Hill
Page Land			
Page Land		250	
Pelzer			
Dixie		400	Thomas Crane, mgr (1921)
Pelzer		400	
Pickens			
Alexander		250	(1927) Film Yearbook
Jefferson			
Pic			Formerly Jefferson
Piedmont			
Star		500	Hale & Boiter, mgrs (1921)
McCormick		200	(1927) Film Yearbook
Piedmont		400	
Ridgeland			
Coastal		300	
Rock Hill			
Pastime			(1921) Cahn and Hill
Imperial		300	(1927) Film Yearbook
Rialto		500	(1927) Film Yearbook
Glynn		300	(1927) Film Yearbook
Capitol		400	
Carolina		300	

Theatre	Location	Seats	Note
Rock Hill (continued)			
Pix	147 W. Oakland Ave.	800	
Stevenson	109 E. Main St.	500	
St. George			
Park		200	(1927) Film Yearbook
St. George			
Lourie	206 N. Parlor Ave.	300	
St. Matthews			
Calhoun		300	
St. Stephen			
Pleasu		250	(1927) Film Yearbook
St. Stephen	1159 S. Main St.	250	Closed, still standing
Salley			
Salley		250	
Saluda			
Pastime		200	(1927) Film Yearbook
Saluda	107 Law Range	300	NRHP
Seneca			
Star		250	(1927) Film Yearbook
Richardson	121 Townville St.	300	
Simpsonville			
Royal	Main St.	300	
Slater			
Slater		300	
Spartanburg			
Lyric	136 East Main St	350	1909
Rialto	136 East Main St	350	1917
Criterion	136 East Main St	350	1934-1940
Grand	139 East Main St	375	1910
Bijou	139 East Main St	375	1915
Lester	146 East Main St	800	1913-1915
Strand	146 East Main St	800	1915-1946
Rex	168 East Main St.	1000	1917-1929
State	168 East Main St	1000	1934-1970
Capri	168 East Main St	600	1970-1971
Palmetto	172 East Main St.	800	1941-1972 NRHP (demolished)

Theatre	Location	Seats	Note
Spartanburg (continued)			
Globe	190 S. Liberty St		African-American (1913)
Montgomery	181 N. Church St.	1000	1925
Carolina	181 N. Church St.	1000	Formerly Montgomery
Dunbar	Short Wofford St	350	African-American c.1926-1930
Union	Short Wofford St	350	African American c.1930-1942
Ritz		500	African American
Springfield			
New			(1921) Cahn and Hill
Springfield		300	
Sullivans Island			
(Also known as Moultrieville)			
Fort Moultrie	1454 Middle St.	100	(1927) Film Yearbook
Fort Theater			
Summerton			
Pastime		200	(1927) Film Yearbook
Gem		300	
Summerville			
Arcade		400	(1927) Film Yearbook
Summerville			
James F. Dean	133 S. Main St.	209	
Sumter			
Carolina		800	
Garden		200	(1927) Film Yearbook
Lyric		300	African American
Rex		500	Mr. Cardoza, mgr (1921)
Victory		200	(1927) Film Yearbook
Sumter		600	
Swansea			
Paramount		600	
Taylors			
Taylors			
Timmonsville			
Dixie			(1921) Cahn and Hill
Garden		250	(1927) Film Yearbook
State		300	Albert Whittemores, mgr. (1939)

Theatre	Location	Seats	Note
Tucapau			
Startex		300	
Union			
Edisonia			
Grand		250	(1927) Film Yearbook
New			
Rialto		500	(1927) Film Yearbook
Union		300	
Duncan			Stewart & Everett, FDY 1965
Varnville			
Varnville		200	W.H. Rentz, mgr (1921)
Strand		300	(1927) Film Yearbook
Wagener			
Wagener		200	
Walhalla			
Strand		400	
Walterboro			
New Era		300	(1927) Film Yearbook
Ritz	329 E. Washington St.	363	Henry Belk Cook, owner
Cook	N. Lucas St.		Henry Belk Cook, owner
Ware Shoals			
Y.M.C.A.		400	
West Columbia			
Dixie	16 State St.	300	
Westminster			
Rex			Geo. Wilson, mgr (1921)
Capitol		280	
Whitmire			
Ideal			(1921) Cahn and Hill
Strand		300	
Williamston			
Star		300	(1927) Film Yearbook
Ritz		400	
Williamston		250	

Theatre	Location	Seats	Note
Williston			
Williston		250	
Winnsboro			
Winnsboro Mills			(1921) Cahn and Hill
Palace		300	(1927) Film Yearbook
Carolina		250	
Fairfield		250	M. Meriwether, mgr. (1938)
Boyd			
Woodruff			
Happyland			(1921) Cahn and Hill
Hollywood		350	
York			
(Also known as Yorkville)			
Starr		350	J. Wing, mgr (1921)
Hollywood			Mr. Fleming, mgr (1938)
Sylvia		350	

Rock Hill Drive-In
Rock Hill

Thanks to Robert Ratterree, Sr., for the photograph of the Rock Hill Drive-In and the wonderful memory he has of it.

"The Rock Hill Drive-In was located on the East side of Rock Hill, about a mile out East Main Street. This theatre showed a lot of kinda shady things from time to time and we heard that it was showing the birth of a baby. Well, we rounded up all the troops and got a car load of young kids off to see "The Wizard" and something we had never seen. We went, and we did see the special feature of the birth of a baby. You talk about a grossed out car load of young'uns leaving a drive-in. To this day, every time I hear about a birth, I think of that drive-in. Some memories just stick with you."

Hall's Drive-In - West Columbia

Alice Drive-In - Columbia

Entrance to South 17 Drive-In in Hardeeville - Members of Greene family adding posters.
Photograph from September, 1950, courtesy Bill Greene

Our friend Bill Greene shared this recently discovered and rare movie poster from 1950. The South 17 Drive-In was operated by Bill's parents William (Bill) and Dolly Greene. The Greene family operated several single screen theaters and drive-ins in South Carolina.

Screen of South 17 Drive-In in Hardeeville

Seabreeze Drive-In - Mount Pleasant
"Just Across the Cooper
At the Dairy Queen"

There is no inclusive list for drive-in theaters in South Carolina. This list is drawn from several sources including *Film Daily Yearbook*, local newspapers, as well as emails and letters from people who visited our website over several years. We apologize if we missed your favorite drive-in.

Anderson	Fox Drive-In
	Skyway Drive-In
	Highway 29 Drive-In
	Viking Outdoor Cinema
Aiken	Fox Drive-In
Andrews	Name Unknown
Barnwell	South Hill Drive-In
Beaufort	Highway 21 Drive-In
	Royal Drive-In
	Greenlawn Drive-In
Bennettsville	By Pass Drive-In
	Star-Lite Drive-In
	Bonds Auto Theater
Camden	Sky-Vue Drive-In
Charleston	Victory Downs Drive-In
	Magnolia Drive-In
	4-Mile Drive-In
Chester	Chester Drive-In
Cheraw	Variety Drive-In
Clio	Clio Drive-In
Clover	York Clover Drive-In
Columbia	Alice Drive-In
	Alta-Vista Drive-In
	Beltline Drive-In
	North 1 Drive-In
	Skyway Drive-In
	Starlite Drive-In
	Sunset Drive-In
	Terrace Drive-In
	Twilight Drive-In
Conway	501 Drive-In
Dillon	301 Drive-In
Easley	Easley Drive-In
Elloree	Elloree Drive-In
Erhardt	Name Unknown

Florence	Palmetto Drive-In	Rock Hill	Fort Roc Drive-In
	Circle Drive-In		Auto Drive-In
Georgetown	Carolina Drive-In		Rock Hill Drive-In
Gloverville	Valley Drive-In	Seneca	Fox Drive-In
Greenville	Augusta Road Drive-In	Spartanburg	Camelot Drive-In
	Belmont Drive-In		Circle South 29 Drive-In
	Cedar Lane Drive-In		Pine Street Extension Drive-In
	Skyland Drive-In		Scenic Drive-In
	White Horse Drive-In		Starlight Drive-In
Greenwood	Mighty Auto Drive-In		Thunderbird Drive-In
Greer	Greer Drive-In		West View Drive-In
	King Cotton Drive-In	St. George	Name Unknown
Hardeeville	South 17 Drive-In	Sumter	New Skyvue Drive-In
Hartsville	Terrace View Drive-In	Taylors	Belmont Drive In
Inman	Moonlite Drive-In	Travelers Rest	Blue Ridge Drive-In
Kershaw	General Kershaw Drive-In	Union	Sunset Drive-In
Kingstree	Kingstree Drive-In	Walterboro	Walterboro Drive-In
	Earl's Drive-In	West Columbia	Hall's Drive-In Theatre
Lake City	East Main Drive-In	Williston	Nu Era Drive-In
Lancaster	Motor In Drive-In	Winnsboro	Winn-Ridge Drive-In
	Town View Drive-In	Yemasee	Name Unknown
Laurens	Eppron Drive-In		
Lexington	#1 Drive-In		
	Ray's Drive-In		
McColl	Unknown Drive-In		
Moncks Corner	Berkeley Drive-In		
	Swamp Fox Drive-In (aka Berkeley)		
Monetta	Monetta Drive-In - OPEN		
Mount Pleasant	Name Unknown		
Mullins	76 Drive-In		
Myrtle Beach	Flamingo Drive-In		
	Myrtle Drive-In		
Newberry	Clover Leaf Drive-In		
New Ellenton	Skyline Drive-In		
North Augusta	Hilltop Drive-In		
North Charleston	North 52 Drive-In		
	Port Drive-In		
	Flamingo Drive-In		
	Gateway Drive-In		
Orangeburg	Orangeburg Drive-In		
	Bon-Air Drive-In		
Pamplico	Name Unknown		
Ridgeland	Ridgeland Drive-In		

Exit sign from the Abbeville Opera House in Abbeville, SC.

15031555R00096

Made in the USA
Lexington, KY
04 May 2012